Rediscovering Northwest Denver

Its History, Its People, Its Landmarks

By Ruth Eloise Wiberg

University Press of Colorado

Photography by Errol Salter (unless otherwise credited)
Typography by Bradford Typographics
Graphic Design by Elizabeth Hickler
Cover Design by Rhonda Pattengill Miller

Published by the University Press of Colorado
P.O. Box 849, Niwot, CO 80544

Library of Congress Cataloging-in-Publication Data
Wiberg, Ruth Eloise.
    Rediscovering Northwest Denver : its history, its
people, its landmarks / by Ruth Eloise Wiberg.
        p.   cm.
    Originally published: Denver : Northwest Denver
Books, c1976.
    Includes bibliographical references and index.
    ISBN 0-87081-372-2 (pbk. : alk. paper)
        1. Historic buildings—Colorado—Denver.
2. Architecture—Colorado—Denver.   3. Denver
(Colo.)—Buildings, structures, etc.   4. Denver
(Colo.)—History.   I. Title.
F784.D48A27   1995
978.8'83—dc20

                                        95-11464
                                          CIP
Sixth printing May 1996

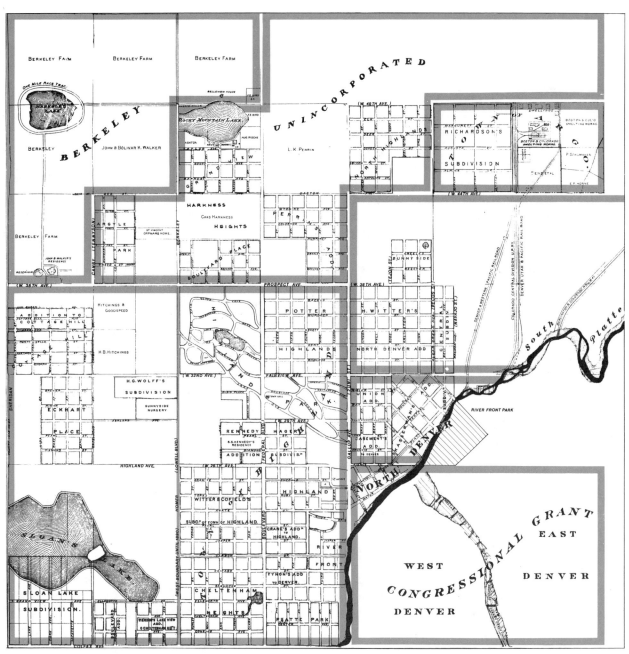

Map of Northwest Denver revised from Rollandet's map of 1885.

Foreword

This new edition of Ruth Wiberg's *Rediscovering Northwest Denver* resurrects a rare, out-of-print bible for Denver's northwest quadrant. Thanks in part to Ruth's book, Northwest Denver is undergoing a renaissance with the rediscovery and restoration of many neighborhoods. Dozens of individual structures and seven districts have earned landmark designation.

For at least three decades, Ruth has helped Northwest Denverites rediscover their roots. Her memories, dating back to childhood, have introduced newcomers and reintroduced us lifelong residents to the characters, to the colorful women and men who climbed up the bluff of the South Platte River to find higher ground.

Ruth's guidebook and history leads us along the old gold rush trails that became major thoroughfares of Northwest Denver. She introduces us to the movers and shakers and takes us into their Victorian mansions. But she also shares with us the lives of blue collar folk in their small bungalows.

Ruth sensitively traces the migrations of various ethnic groups who have lived, loved, worked, fought, and moved into Colorado's most fascinating melting pot. She uses churches as focal points: All Saint's Episcopal for the English; Asbury Methodist (now Korean) for the Cornish and Welsh; St. Patrick's for the Irish; Mount Carmel for the Italians; and Our Lady of Guadalupe for Hispanics. Her chapter, "Towns on the Perimeter of Highlands," includes the town of Brooklyn on West Colfax Avenue where Jewish pioneers settled among Orthodox shuls and Kosher shops.

Argo, the smelter town named for the ship in which Jason sailed after the golden fleece in Greek mythology, hosted hardworking Slavs and Germans from Russia. Berkeley, in the northwest corner of Northwest Denver, became a haven for splendid city parks and Regis University. Ruth's extensive coverage of Elitch Gardens will guide redevelopment of the North Denver site after Colorado's most storied amusement park moved in 1995 to the Central Platte Valley.

Ruth's classic account revives Northwest Denver's neighborhood spirits. I have had the honor of representing Northwest Denver as a state representative or senator since 1971. During that time I have worked with Ruth and used her fine book for neighborhood tours that I conduct, often with my sidekick Tom Noel. One of the many advantages of this classic is the suggested self-guided tours you will find on the final pages.

So, dear readers, be delighted, be inspired by the treasure you hold in your hands, your guide to rediscovering Northwest Denver.

Dennis Gallagher
State Senator and Assistant Professor of
Communication Arts, Regis University

Contents

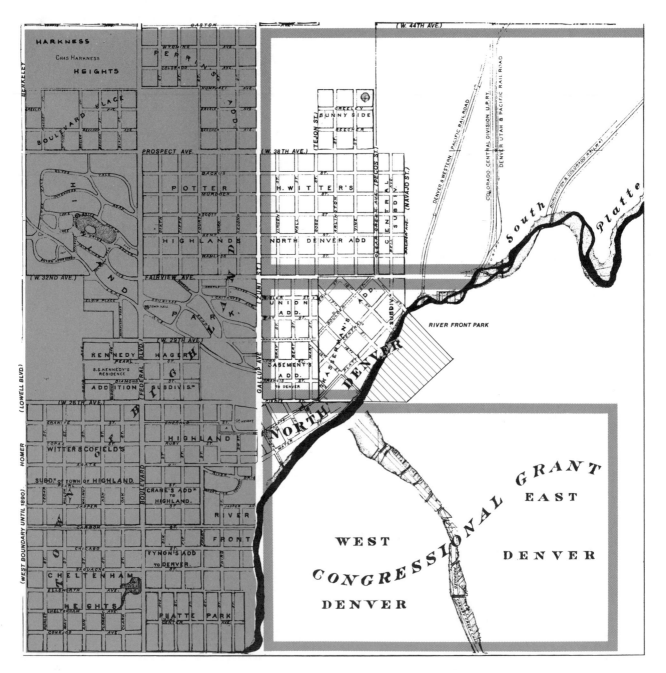

The Original North Denver

Its founding

The possibility of gold in those steep hills and gullies across the frozen South Platte river was remote, but the two men were not searching for gold. One of them, General William Larimer, was a land promoter. He started towns. Some which he had laid out in Kansas had grown, more had not. D. C. Collier, who was with him, was temporarily sharing Larimer's dirt-roofed log cabin in the sparse collection of shacks and tents, which Larimer had optimistically named Denver City.

The desire to start another town once again tugged at Larimer as he looked across the river. The land was there for the taking — or staking — so why not? (Indian claims didn't count.) So, that day, December 11, 1858, the two men crossed the South Platte River near the mouth of Cherry Creek. Larimer wrote his wife (*Larimer Reminiscences,* privately published, reprinted 1918), "We had a cold bath. I waded with my boots on and after crossing I put on dry buffalo shoes, but feared my feet were frozen. I took off my coat and put my feet in the sleeves and Mr. Collier rubbed until he restored circulation. The river was frozen with the exception of about thirty feet, which we waded in three feet of water. Collier took off his trousers. We had a blanket which we lay on the ice to change our clothes."

The two men went on to plat a town on the hilly slopes. They named it Highland. (This name, without an *s* at the end, should not be confused with Highlands, a different area that was founded at a later date.)

Adventurers and gold seekers had traveled and would travel hundreds of miles across unclaimed plains and many rivers to reach this confluence of the South Platte and Cherry Creek. Now Larimer was gambling that they would cross still another river, this wide and shallow South Platte, and would pay good money for lots on those brown hills dotted with gray-green yucca and prickly pear cactus. They had to cross sometime if they wanted to reach the peaks beyond, where Larimer was sure rich gold deposits lay. Some surely would gamble on land as easily as on gold.

Larimer and Collier waded back to Denver City. This was one of the towns he founded that was destined to survive and grow, with a street named after him. Across Cherry Creek from his hamlet, where the creek met the river, lay Auraria, which boasted a number of dwellings at the time Larimer's small party had arrived from Kansas a month ago. So now there were three townsites clustered along the streams, Denver City, Auraria, and Highland.

In a couple of months a ferry was chartered to operate across the Platte and on May 2, 1859, the *Rocky Mountain News* reported: "A large number of new houses are going up in Highland. Among them we notice one being built by W. H. Middaugh, 30 feet by 82 feet, two stories high. It is designed for a hotel."

The ferry was replaced by a bridge in January 1860, which helped Highland grow to a point where it had 42 voters in an election held later that month.

Denver and Auraria, the two fledgling towns east of the Platte and on opposite sides of Cherry Creek, were

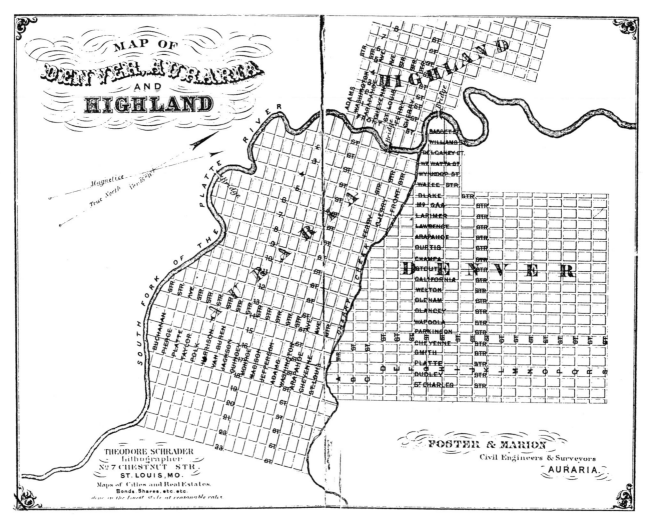

The three towns of the Platte-Cherry Creek confluence, 1859

hating, fighting rivals over which would become the dominant town. In 1859 the two towns decided that for either to survive they must join. They included in this merger the town of Highland, which after 1861 was officially known as North Denver or North Division, although commonly called Highland.

Denver City and Auraria, the Commercial Emporium of the Pikes Peak Gold Regions in 1859 reported: "It will be seen by a glance at the accompanying map that a third town is springing up on the left bank of the South Platte immediately opposite Auraria and Denver. It is being called Highland from the steady gradual rise of its area from the bank of the river towards the bluffs that form its outer limits. A better and more picturesque site cannot

8

be found anywhere. Near the river it is almost level and appears to be especially created for the business portion of the town, while the southern slopes of the bluffs that form part of it afford high healthy airy places of residences, with a full and splendid view."

The South Platte at that time had two deep bends east of the mouth of Cherry Creek — bends which swept in as far as the present site of the Union Station. The river itself straightened these oxbow curves, aided by man and the railroads when they arrived. The first Congressional Grant of 1860 gave little land to North Denver, with the north boundary lying at about the present West 26th Avenue. In 1864 the Congressional Grant was amended, carrying the north boundary to what is now West 32nd Avenue, and the Session Laws of 1883 extended it to West 44th Avenue. The west boundary of North Denver was always Zuni Street (then called Gallup Avenue), and the south and east boundaries were the river.

Trails across the Highland Hills

Mountain men, Indians, prospectors, gamblers, adventurers, traders — all trekked these high prairies. The trails wandered wherever the mud or the snowbanks were the least deep, where the hills were less steep and the water holes more prevalent. The extension of the Overland Trail towards Virginia Dale crossed the river at 15th Street and climbed the hills to the north, stopping at a watering hole which is now Rocky Mountain Lake at West 46th Avenue and Federal Boulevard. It followed the high ridge to cross Clear Creek at Jim Baker's ferry, just west of Tennyson Street (Long, Margaret, *The Smoky Hill Trail*, W. H. Kistler Stationery Co., 1943, pg. 202).

Other trails scattered across the prairies toward Boulder Diggings, toward the now vanished town of Arapahoe on Clear Creek, toward the toll road up Golden Gate Canyon to Black Hawk and Central City. One probably crossed the Platte at about 7th Street or 9th Street, slowly crawled up the hills and stopped at a stage station at about the present West 26th Avenue and Eliot Street. This building has been razed now, but hitching rings imbedded in the tree trunks showed until the trees were cut down.

A road, known sometimes as the Prospect Trail, sometimes the North Golden Road, to Arapahoe City, Golden, and the mining camps to the west, followed what became Prospect Avenue and still later West 38th Avenue. The South Golden Road became West Colfax.

Life on the Denver frontier

Denver City and Auraria were typical shoot-it-out towns, and at first had only vigilante law and order enforcement, with quick sentences of hanging handed down by a People's Court. The numerous shootings and murders were for the usual reasons of jealousy, robbery, claim jumping, drunken arguments. The few women in those quick-trigger days were afraid to go into their gardens without a shotgun. One three-day "war" was fought over a jumped claim; another day-long reign of shootings and panic swept the town because of some stolen turkeys. North Denver apparently had no murders of its own, but some of the dregs of Denver's affairs affected this section.

March 5, 1860 there was a genteel dinner of prominent men at one of Denver's best hotels, The Broadwell. These men sat down to a meal served on linens in a room that was plastered and painted and perhaps papered, in the first thoroughly finished frame building in the city. They were gentlemen, dressed in black broadcloth with fine white shirts and broad cravats. Wine was served and toasts were offered. L. W. Bliss, acting governor of the territory, proposed a toast which included anti-slavery remarks. This angered Dr. J. S. Stone, a member of the legislative assembly and Judge of the Miners' Court. There was a violent argument, culminating with a glass of wine thrown in Dr. Stone's face. Inevitably, Dr. Stone challenged Governor Bliss to a duel. The site chosen was the north (Highland) end of the 15th Street bridge. At three in the afternoon, March 7, 1860, the two men faced each other at a distance of 30 paces with shotguns loaded with ball. Dr. Stone fell at the first shot, mortally wounded, although he lingered in agonizing pain for five months before dying.

Hangings for murder, ordered by the People's Court, were carried out at various spots in and around the towns. The last one of these executions was of a Patrick

Waters, who had murdered a companion near Fort Lupton and had hidden the body. He ran away but was captured soon and was hanged on a gallows hurriedly erected at the north end of the 15th Street bridge, approximately the same site as that chosen for the Stone-Bliss duel.

Early real estate transactions

Activity in North Denver followed the ups and downs of central Denver. It was slowed by grasshopper plagues, droughts, and the isolation of the area by the Civil War and by Indian raids on the plains. It was accelerated by every strike of gold in the mountains and the influx of more and more people.

Highland (or North Denver) was still largely open country in 1866 when various Masonic groups and the Independent Order of Odd Fellows, both of which had organized early in Denver, purchased a tract of 40 acres on the high steep slopes north of the Platte to be used as a cemetery. This tract, which is bounded today by West 32nd Avenue, Tejon Street, West 29th Avenue, and Zuni Street, was known as Acacia Cemetery. Seven years after it was started an item in the *Denver Daily Tribune* of October 29, 1873 stated, "The removal of these burying grounds would take away an eyesore to what is soon to be the very heart of a populous and prosperous part of Denver. The high handsomely located grounds would be of ready sale and eagerly caught up for building purposes."

The lodges agreed to sell the property. They transferred the bodies from Acacia Cemetery to an area near 9th and York Streets, which, on Edward Rollandet's map of 1885, shows Old City Cemetery, Catholic Cemetery, Hebrew Cemetery, Odd Fellows Cemetery, Masonic Cemetery, and one marked simply Cemetery. Later a third move was made of the bodies to Riverside. After having been buried three times, those bones could have been restless. Is it imagination that makes people who have their houses on that hillside in North Denver insist that ghosts wander and wail about their homes? Others on that site swore that when their basements were dug human bones which had been missed in the move were found.

Real estate dealings in early Denver — and North

Denver was no exception — could be rather casual matters, with titles changing hands over the gambling tables, or traded for a good horse and saddle, or for a shotgun and a slab of bacon or sack of flour. Some abstracts show transfers "For L and A," which means "for love and affection."

Matters became more businesslike as the town grew. October 29, 1873, the *Denver Daily Tribune* reported: "A look around the North Side shows that part of Denver to be pushing ahead in a very surprising and handsome manner. New neat buildings appear on every hand, and the several stores are doing a lively business. Capelli's new hotel and hall, built at a cost of some $15,000, the Chrisman Mill turning out its 100 sacks of flour per day, Bender's Soap Works and Soggs Vinegar Factory are among the enterprises worthy of mention."

Another enterprise which was doing exceedingly well on the North Side was the Rocky Mountain Brewery started in 1859, the first brewery between the Mississippi and the Pacific Coast. After various owners and partners, John Good became the proprietor by 1864. He was joined by Phillip Zang who came to Denver in 1869. These two industrious Germans turned out about a dozen barrels of good beer a day, which Zang delivered in an old wheelbarrow. In a couple of years Zang purchased Good's share in the business and, although the buildings were badly damaged by fire in 1874 and again in 1881, they were always built up again, bigger and handsomer than before. Zang sold his holdings in the company in 1889, but it continued under other ownership to a peak of 175,000 barrels a day in 1917, a $3,000,000 concern. Most of the buildings have been victims of subsequent fires, so that all that remains today at its location of 7th and Water Streets is the stable with its round and square brick towerettes, presently used as a factory.

Phillip Zang had built his large home near the brewery, a spot now covered by the Valley Highway. In 1902 or 1903 he moved to an elaborate mansion at East 7th Avenue and Clarkson Street, which is still a showplace, owned at present by the Colorado Mission of the Church of Latter Day Saints. Both Zang and Good had many other interests besides the brewery, and became giants of business in Colorado.

Zang had brought over from Germany a George

Views of 1890, O. O. Howard, Jr.

Zang Brewery

Schmidt to be his head brewmaster. Schmidt built a large house at 7th and Water Streets which still stands, a two-story red brick of ten or more rooms. It had thirteen inch thick walls. On the back porch was a large galvanized beer tank so that Schmidt might always be able to serve the best to his guests. The dining room had an ingenious heating system — water pipes ran through the fireplace to become heated and then followed the baseboard around the room. The city government in recent years condemned this heating as dangerous. The house has some interesting grapevine carvings above the front entrance (one wonders why it isn't barley sheaves) and did have some beautiful leaded glass windows and fine interior woodwork, much of which was stolen by a so-called collector when the house was temporarily vacated.

Other early North Denverites

Only a few of the many interesting or influential people of North Denver can be described in detail, because of space.

An early resident was Dr. William Smedley, a dentist and Quaker, who came first to Auraria in 1870 for his health. He brought his bride from Pennsylvania to Colorado in 1872 and established a family home on Ninth Street in Auraria, now the oldest and only frame of the Ninth Street Park homes. Dr. Smedley found Auraria too crowded and polluted with urban and industrial odors. He studied wind currents carefully to locate a spot where the air was clear and clean and selected a hill at what is now West 35th Avenue and Pecos Street in North Denver, which was away from the drifting smelter

11

Home of George Schmidt, brewmaster at Zang Brewery

Home of Dr. and Mrs. William Smedley (now demolished)

smoke. He was convinced this area would develop into a fine residential district because of the air and the view. About 1888 he built a handsome red brick two-story home at 925 Clear Creek Avenue (later changed to 3525 Pecos). The house had been razed and the block is occupied by the North Side Community Center. The house, typical of the better homes of that time, had a parlor, back parlor, library, dining room, kitchen, six bedrooms, and a big attic. There was a deck at the top, surrounded by a decorative iron fence, from which the family could view the whole growing city. The family had its own artesian well, a fine garden, lawn, and trees, and even a tennis court. A large stable housed their carriage horses, their own cows, and chickens. Dr. Smedley established a dental clinic in the city which is still in existence. He was active in educational circles and served on the school board for many years. A Denver Public School built in 1902 at 43rd and Shoshone is named the Smedley School.

Charles A. Wheeler built a large home on a high hill directly overlooking the Platte Valley and the city opposite, at West 28th Avenue and Wyandot Street. Mr.

Smedley School, 1902

Hallie Bond

Charles A. Wheeler built one of the early "Denver squares"

William Coors chose North Denver instead of Golden

Wheeler was an accountant and comptroller of various railroad companies in Denver. Wheeler, who had numerous real estate holdings, had come to Colorado in 1860, and later was a sergeant major in the Civil War. Hall's *History of Colorado* (Hall, Frank, *History of Colorado*, Blakely Printing Co., 1895) says: "Mr. Wheeler is rated by railway men as one of the most accomplished, accurate and efficient accountants in the service. By the people of Denver, among whom he has so long resided, he is esteemed as one of the most valuable citizens." The home, built in 1890, broke away from the traditional Victorian style of towers, gingerbread and wrought iron, to be a three-story house of square lines without exterior ornamentation, a style known throughout the country as a "Denver square,"although not with the dormered hip roof of that style. It was a house of about twenty rooms, long ago turned into apartments, but which is still prominent on its hill above the north end of the Speer viaduct.

North Denver attracted members of other families whose names became familiar to all Coloradans. While Adolph Coors lived in Golden where his brewery and porcelain works were located, his brother William, who was associated with the brewery business, lived in North Denver at 3325 Goss Street (now Tejon). Boys of that time remember him as having the nicest house on the block and as being the nicest man in the block. It seems that although Mr. Coors had three non-tomboyish daughters, he brought home hop sacks which he stuffed with straw to be used as gym mats, and in the corner of his backyard he put in rings, bars, and jumps, for the use of the boys in the neighborhood.

Another man made North Denver the focus of the entire country for two months in the fall of 1895. His name was Francis Schlatter, a former shoe cobbler, a small compact man, dressed — according to realistic observers — in a clean blue calico shirt with a piece of white linen over his breast, blue denim jacket and overalls, and pepper and salt socks. He had long flowing brown hair, parted in the middle and covering his ears, a soft brown beard, Jewish features and kindly blue eyes. He was an unpretentious man, a simple man, with a sincere belief that he had an unusual gift, that of faith healing.

Schlatter had been a shoe cobbler on the east side of town, but he gave up his money-losing business and traveled to New Mexico. There he was reputed to have healed a young blind girl. When word reached Denver of this miracle, interested persons sent for him and lodged him with Edward L. Fox, a former alderman of the city of Denver and a successful grain and coal merchant, who lived at 625 Witter Street. Witter Street became either Quivas or Raritan; number 625 would probably be in the present 3200 block.

In those more unsophisticated days, words of Schlatter's prowess spread rapidly. Some swore he wore luminous white robes and they declared this to be the second coming of Christ. Others called it a hoax. Nevertheless thousands came every day to see him. Lines of people formed at the gate to Fox' residence, the crippled in wheelchairs, on crutches, canes, stretchers, all to have this miracle man lay his hands on them and say a few words of prayer. Wealthy local people came in carriages, others on foot, on horseback, or on the cable car. Newspapers all over the country carried stories, although actual cases of healing were hard to find. Eastern firms hired special trains to bring their employees to him. Specials also came in from other towns all over the Rocky Mountain Region. Wealthy from the east, the west, the south came in private railroad cars. Schlatter, standing for many long hours at the front gate, took each one in turn, regardless of station in life or urgency.

Except for the few words uttered over each seeker, he spoke little. He seldom ate, saying he was fed by the spirit. He slept only short hours, for he spent long evenings, assisted by Mr. Fox, answering thousands of letters. The post office estimated he received as many as 8000 letters daily. Many people sent him handkerchiefs to be blessed, and he said a prayer over each before he slipped it into a return envelope.

Opportunists sold handkerchiefs, imprinted with his picture, to the thousands gathered at the gate. Others sold places in the long lines. But Schlatter himself never accepted money from anyone.

Through October and November he continued his blessings to the people. He seemed to be growing very tired as the air became chill with approaching winter. His expression of weariness and dedication deepened. Doctors said he looked as if he were suffering from liver disease.

One November day a white horse appeared in the stable of Fox' hay and grain business. The prosaic said it was a retired fire horse; others spoke in whispers of a small ass found in a village two thousand years ago. And then, one morning, Fox found a note saying, "My mission is finished. Father takes me home. Goodbye." Schlatter and the white horse were gone.

Almost immediately from various and widely separated places about the country came reports that Schlatter was there. The most authentic stories indicated he rode south through New Mexico. In various towns people saw him, spoke to him, gave him gifts — a brass

17

August Rische's
little cottages

Hallie Bond

staff, a Bible, a watch. Here the odyssey seemed to fade away.

Meantime, a rather tawdry sequel was taking place. Fox, who had neglected his business more and more to help Schlatter, and who seemed to become erratic in his behavior, disappeared. He was found in Louisville, Kentucky, preaching on the street corners, apparently feeling himself a disciple of Schlatter's. With him was a woman faith healer, going by the name of Amanda Fox. Mrs. Fox, in Denver, his legal wife, had him arrested for violation of the Mann Act so that he might be brought back to Denver and declared insane.

Nothing further had been heard of Schlatter, although imitators continued to appear in various places. Five years after he left Denver it was learned that in 1896 — less than a year after he disappeared from Colorado, a body had been found in a lonely cave in the northern state of Sonora, Mexico. Beside it were a brass staff, a Bible, and a watch, all gifts presented to Schlatter as he traveled south through New Mexico. The story of Francis Schlatter, the shoemaker with a mission, was closed.

August Rische was a man of another kind of vision. He was one of the two prospectors whom H. A. W.

Denver Public Schools

The two early Bryant School buildings

Tabor, Colorado's famous silver king, grubstaked into a fortune for himself. Rische had also been a cobbler, and came from Missouri to Colorado to find gold and did. He and his partner, George Hook, grudgingly given whiskey and food by Tabor, in return for a share of whatever they found, discovered the fabulous Little Pittsburgh mine at Leadville. Hook sold his share of the profits immediately to Tabor, but Rische kept his, approximately $400,000. He and his wife moved to Denver and into its society circles. He had an elaborate home at Colfax and Sher-

man, where the State Office Building now stands.

Rische had made real estate investments in the northwest sector of the city and about 1884 moved to 1659 Boulder Street, a house which has now been torn down. Two small brick cottages, with high peaked roofs, carved stone lintels, and lacy wooden millwork about the eaves and the gables, built in 1886, which were next door to the Rische home and which he owned, are still standing.

Rische was always sure he would make another fabu-

Webster School built in 1892

lous strike, but he never did. He and Tabor both lost their money in the Panic of 1893. When he died in 1910, Rische's fortunes had declined to the point where he was working as a watchman at the State Capitol.

The schools

To the early settlers, education was one of the most important essentials. In the spring of 1872 a one-room frame school was built at the southeast corner of 15th and Central Streets, which would be in the middle of the Valley Highway today. By the time the school opened that fall, the population had outgrown the building and classes had to be held outdoors. From then on, there was a race between the school board and the increasing crop of children, with the children always winning.

In the early 1880's the Bryant School at (now) West

This building combined two schools

36th Avenue and Shoshone Street, was built. It was a small building with only two rooms. The school board (Arapahoe County District #17) managed to find enough money in 1883 to add four rooms to the original two. By 1890 the population was exploding all over the district, and another Bryant School was built on the large grounds on which the six-room school stood. Two years later Webster School was erected just six blocks away at West 36th and Lipan. Forty years later, in 1930, the two schools, Bryant and Webster, were combined into a new building on the grounds of the old Bryant. The combined school, with the name of Bryant-

21

Horace Mann Junior High School

Webster, is an attractive one with American Indian motifs worked into the brick, and was designed by G. Meredith Musick.

North Side High School was started in 1883. Its story in detail is included in the section on Highlands. The concept of junior high schools was presented to the public in the 1920's, to serve the 7th, 8th and 9th grades, and Horace Mann Junior High was built at 41st and Navajo in 1931, with an addition in 1956. It is of light brick with ornamentation of the same brick. There were also parochial institutions, both large and small, but their story must be a separate one from this.

Transportation to downtown Denver

Access to the city was essential but difficult for the residents of North Denver. At various times in the early years, there were wooden bridges across the Platte at 7th, 9th, 14th, 15th, and 19th Streets. Some of these were replaced in the 1880's with iron bridges. The one at 19th Street, an intriguing one with rather delicate and graceful ornamentation, is the only one of these wrought iron bridges still standing in 1976. The 19th Street bridge marks the site of an early settlement of Volga-German immigrants, a place chosen because they found it a spot where the river was accessible for them to do their laundry.

North Denver was served by both horse cars and cable cars. A horse car traveled north on Clear Creek Avenue (now Pecos) as far as the town of Argo, which was at 44th Avenue. This was a leisurely informal ride on which the operators and the horses knew the stops and the passengers and would wait if a regular customer wasn't quite ready when they arrived. Coming home from town, people carried a fascinating array of items, even furniture, from their shopping trips. Cable cars

Cable car
on 16th Street trestle

19th Street
Wrought Iron Bridge, 1880's

Cable car barns on Zuni Street
(Gallup Ave.)

were pulled slowly up the steep hills after crossing the growing railroad tracks and the river by way of a wooden trestle at 16th Street. One cable line ran north on Tejon Street to about 41st Avenue. Others ran to the cable car terminal and barn at West 30th and Zuni Street (which was then Gallup Avenue).

For any further transportation, families used buggies, wagons, or carriages. After crossing the bridge on their way downtown, they still had to drive across the railroad tracks, steadying skitterish horses as they waited for long slow trains to pass or switch, always trying to avoid a cinder that might float into the eye, and always smelling the acrid dirty train smoke that swirled about.

The coming of business districts

Because of the busy traffic crossing the 15th Street bridge, an impressive business district was built up along 15th Street from Platte Street to Boulder Street.

In the city directory of 1882 a North Denver Hotel is listed at the northwest corner of Platte and 15th, and in 1883 a Highland Hotel is shown at the southeast corner of Platte and 15th, either of which might have been a brothel. At the northeast corner of the same intersection the Olinger Mortuary was started in 1890. The family lived in the basement. When John Olinger, the founder, died, his wife moved the business to 16th and Boulder in 1909 and managed both family and business for many years.

The North Denver Bank was in an impressive red brick building at the northwest corner of 15th and Central. This bank was one of the dozen banks which closed in the Silver Panic of 1893, but it paid all depositors in full.

On the northeast side of 15th from Central to Boulder the Marquis Block and the Slockett Building were and are prominent, made especially interesting by the cast iron pillars along the front of the buildings. These struc-

24

King and McDowell
Building detail

North Denver Bank

Souvenir Album, Compiled by W. A. Barbot

Marquis Block

Hallie Bond

Slockett Building detail

Hallie Bond

Some of eight brownstone
duplexes on West 28th Ave.

tures apparently were built by men who made money in mining but later invested in more stable real estate and prosaic groceries and meat markets. On the two sides of this block were a pharmacy, a fancy grocery, a general mercantile store, real estate and insurance offices, and two furniture stores. At the center of the west side of the block, at 2528-15th Street (now a vacant lot) was Tabor Volunteer Hose Company #5.

Just around the corner, on West 28th Avenue from Vallejo to Umatilla are eight brownstone duplexes built in the 1890s, fascinating in appearance, although their history is not known.

In 1898 Hose Companies #5 and #7 are both listed at the corner of 32nd, Shoshone, and Erie Streets. This location, at the foot of a steep hill, was a poor choice for horses which were intended to take off with the fire wagons at a dead run. Therefore, a new building was erected at West 36th and Tejon in 1909, which is also

now replaced. The old structure at 32nd and Erie, with its round corner towerettes and large arched doors, which made it resemble a fort, was for many years the Tivoli Terrace, a night club, and at present is an apartment house.

Other small business clusters were scattered about North Denver, especially along streetcar lines or at their terminals. Along Gallup Avenue (Zuni) between Ashland Avenue (now West 29th) and Fairview Avenue (now West 32nd), across the street from the cable car terminal, a number of office and business buildings were put up. By 1890 a four-story brick building, with sandstone trim, was erected by Tallmadge and Boyer just north of Ashland Avenue. Tallmadge and Boyer also had a grocery and a six-unit two-story townhouse building on Wyandot in the same block. Their business building on Gallup housed a large dry goods store, a grocery, and the printing and editorial offices of the

Bob Bond

Fire station at West 32nd and Erie

Detail of ornate brick trim

Tallmadge and Boyer business block

Hallie Bond

Tallmadge and Boyer
townhouse complex

Highland Chief, a newspaper of this part of northwest Denver which ran from 1890 to the 1920's. There was also a popular saloon owned by a Mr. Goldsmith, a handsome man who dressed beautifully, wearing a fancy silk vest with a huge watch chain across it and carrying a gold headed cane. Next to this building was the Romeo Building at the corner of present West 30th and Zuni, distinguished by a minaret tower at the corner and bay windows in the second floor offices or apartments. There was a drug store in this building.

Small groceries, bakeries, shoe repair shops, feed stores, notion stores, milliner shops, blacksmith shops,

coal and ice houses, and saloons were dotted here and there in the North Denver area. Since transportation was by either horse or "shank's mare" (as being afoot was called), small grocery stores were numerous. These might be called "ma and pa" businesses in today's idiom, but they were really "ma, pa, and the kids," for the children had many duties — sweeping out the store, shoveling snow off the sidewalks (if there were sidewalks), sacking potatoes, sugar, and flour, refilling the pickle barrel or the cracker barrel, or putting a fresh "spud" on a kerosene spout to keep it from leaking. The older son or, unusual for that day, the oldest daughter

One townhouse entrance

Hallie Bond

Romeo Building

delivered groceries in a light spring wagon. Sometimes he would drive around in the morning to take orders, delivering them in the afternoon. Some people had standing orders. Grocers gave a Christmas turkey to charge customers who paid their bills promptly, and usually each payday children could count on a bag of chocolates when father tallied up with the grocer.

Early migrations to the Platte-Cherry Creek junction

The first trickle of gold seekers and soldiers of fortune of the late 1850's swelled to a brief deluge in the 1860's.

This slowed to a few drops during the years of the Civil War and the Indian raids on the plains. Following the war, gold seekers were not the only settlers swelling a new wave of migration; merchants also came to supply the gold diggers with every need or desire. The first railroad came through from the east in 1870. By the time statehood was conferred on the territory in 1876, migration to the Rockies was an established fact. People came seeking riches, a new way of life, or health.

English, German, Scots, Welsh and Cornish, as well as a multitude from the eastern and southern states, were among the first to try to civilize the frontier. There were so many Germans that from 1877 to 1899 Colorado

All Saints Episcopal
Church (now Chapel
of Our Merciful Savior)

Hallie Bond

35

statutes required that laws be published in German as well as in English and Spanish. Many of these Germans settled in North Denver, possibly because of the large number of their nationality employed by Zang and the other breweries along the Platte. For a few years there was a German Methodist Church at West 27th and Vallejo Streets, and a German Baptist Church was farther north, at Jason Street and West 39th, in 1898.

All Saints Episcopal Church represented the home church to many of the English speaking people. In 1874 it was organized as a mission of the pioneer downtown Episcopal Church, St. John in the Wilderness. The members of this mission parish met in a small building for some years. In 1890 the red brick building at (now) West 32nd Avenue and Wyandot, with its graceful spire, interesting wainscoted and beamed ceiling, and colorful rose window, became home to the parish. In 1961 a new building was erected at West 37th Avenue and Yates Street. The older structure was retained under the same rector and known as the Chapel of Our Merciful Savior. (See same name, page 60, Section II.)

Welsh and Cornish miners had worked in the silver mines of the mountain communities. When silver was demonetized in 1893, causing most silver mines to close, many of these people moved to Denver, and a large number settled in North Denver, clustered around All Saints Church. These families from Wales and Cornwall were by no means wealthy, but they were proud and independent and worked at whatever was available in order to keep their families together. If the mining had played out, they would pursue other lines.

Another imposing Protestant structure, which served the English speaking people of North Denver, marks the skyline as one approaches North Denver from downtown. This is Asbury United Methodist Church, a building of gray and red stone, designated as a landmark by the Denver Landmark Preservation Commission. It has a square open tower, beautiful wooden doors, stained glass windows, and a sanctuary ceiling in the form of a cross. It was designed by Franklin Kidder, an architect noted for his Denver church buildings of those Victorian years. The congregation was organized in 1880 and met in a frame building at what is now 16th and Boulder Streets. The stone edifice, at West 30th Avenue and Vallejo Street, was built in 1890. It houses

the oldest pipe organ in continual use in Colorado, an organ which was built in 1875 by a Denver factory for Temple Emmanuel and later sold to Asbury.

At the time Asbury was built, it was noted that there were twelve other churches in this section of North Denver, ten of them with their own buildings. All the other Protestant congregations erected buildings, then built large ones at other locations on the North Side. Later some moved to the suburb of Highlands to the west. Others merged or discontinued when their buildings burned or their parishioners moved away.

A Friends, or Quaker, Church was built near the north edge of the city, at West 41st Avenue and present Shoshone in 1899, and was occupied by them until 1954, when they built a new edifice at West 46th Avenue and Eliot. The older building has been taken over by a Ukrainian Church with Byzantine rites, which serves a group of much later immigrants who fled Europe during and after World War II.

A new wave of migrants

Seeking a new, although very different, life in the west, came a people during the 1890's and early 1900's, much different from those who had arrived earlier. They were the poor and often unschooled, driven from their European homelands by drouth, depression, overcrowding, or military conscription. In the new world they were urged to go as far west as their money would carry them, where mining, a building boom, construction of railroads, and many demands from a burgeoning population promised work for everyone. Swedes, Poles, Russians, Irish, and Italians followed where earlier migrants had laid the foundations.

A large Irish settlement developed in lower North Denver near the railroads where so many of them worked. To these Irish, in a land and environment very different from home, the church was the one thing that was familiar, and for these loyal Catholics it formed the center of their lives. Bishop Machebeuf established St. Patrick's parish in 1883. It was the pioneer Catholic church for all of Northwest Denver, comprising originally all the territory north of the Platte River. Seven parishes were eventually formed from the original St. Patrick's, as the northwest area built up. The first St.

Asbury United Methodist
Church dominates the
view of North Denver

a new St. Patrick's along these Franciscan lines at West 33rd and Pecos Street. The cornerstone was laid September 15, 1907, but the church was not completed until three years later.

Father Carrigan evidently did not go through all the church-specified channels in the financing and building, which infuriated Bishop Nicholas Matz. There followed a stormy battle which ran seventeen months between Father Carrigan and Bishop Matz. Newspapers avidly reported all the Bishop's charges of insubordination, contempt for authority, contumacy, grave disobedience, thievery, lying, defiance of church laws, illegally holding church property, open rebellion. This finally climaxed in an open letter from the bishop to be read in all Catholic pulpits, excommunicating Father Carrigan. Some priests refused to read it. Father Carrigan read it in his pulpit but refused to accept the excommunication. He countered with charges against the bishop of theft, lying, simony, abuse of power, maladministration, forgery. The newspapers were relishing every bit of the scandal.

Ecclesiastic suits and civil suits were filed. Almost all of his two thousand parishioners remained intensely loyal to Father Carrigan, as did many prominent Catholics about the city and numerous other priests. The Ancient Order of Hibernians praised him for his manly priestly stand, and charged the bishop with jealousy, hatred, the spirit of revenge, and an unchristian spirit. The Knights of St. John, which included both Irish and German, passed resolutions in favor of Father Carrigan.

Eventually, through the efforts of many, the Apostolic Delegate effected a compromise and charges and suits were dropped. Father Carrigan was not excommunicated but he did accept a transfer to Glenwood Springs. He died there in 1938. He was beloved and mourned by Catholics all over the state and especially by the Irish of North Denver to whom he had given a church home away from the homeland.

Close after the Irish came the Italian migrants. By the later 1880's many had reached the west. In Denver they saw the Catholic church, St. Patrick's, close to the railroad tracks, surrounded by small inexpensive housing, and, more especially, close to the rich river bottoms of the Platte. Many of these Italians were from the

Patrick's building was at the corner of Wanless and Bell Avenue (now West 33rd Avenue and Osage Street). This building was later used as the St. Patrick's School and at present is a restaurant.

Father Joseph P. Carrigan came to St. Patrick's when he was only 26, about 1885, and stayed over 25 stormy years. The parishioners, Irish, German, and Anglo, found great spiritual guidance with Father Carrigan, but certainly his pastorate was flavored with impulsiveness and fiery stubbornness.

Father Carrigan went to California in 1907 to study Franciscan missions, and returned to Denver fired with plans to build a similar one, not only on the architectural style, but to develop it into a mission, teaching Catholics and non-Catholics alike. Accordingly he built

St. Patrick's was built
for early Irish immigrants

agricultural south of Italy. Those Platte lands were ideal for vegetable farming, and the southern Italians settled all along the river, north as far as Welby.

The Italians were of two sorts, those from the north of the country who were industrial workers, those from the south who were farmers. They were divided by provincial rivalry, united by the fact that they were all Italians. They clung together. In some cases the men of whole villages migrated to America, to send for their families later. Often the family included grandparents, brothers, sisters, nieces, nephews, and cousins.

They left serious economic unrest and depression in Italy. They were poor in their home country, and they came to the fabled Land of Promise in unbelievably crowded vermin-infested steerage. As soon as they stepped onto American soil they were faced with prejudice. Most of the immigrants up to that day had been fair-skinned and either able to speak English or to learn it quickly. Now came these dark unschooled poor, speaking a strange language. They were looked down upon, called derogatory names.

The first few who arrived in Denver attended St. Patrick's Church. But the Irish Catholic Church was not the Italian church, and an Italian could not feel rapport with a priest with whom he couldn't speak. As more and more of their countrymen came to swell the Italian population, they decided to build their own national church. Father Carrigan reluctantly helped establish the new parish, which is officially named Mount Carmel *Italian* Church. It is located at West 36th Avenue and Navajo Street and was organized in 1894.

Bishop Matz' choice of a priest, Father Mariano Lepore, did not please some of the parishioners although he was an Italian. They accused him of base immorality with certain women; and some men in the parish forbade their wives, sisters, and daughters to speak to him. According to newspaper pictures, he was a handsome man with dark curly hair, and the charisma that attracted women shows through the photographs.

In August, 1898 the brick veneer frame church building of Mount Carmel was burned to the ground, obviously the work of an arsonist. At the height of the fire the priest dramatically fainted and women gathered about him, crying hysterically.

Father Lepore made plans to build a new sanctuary at the same location, to be of sandstone and marble. By now parishioners were split into two factions, and petitions were presented to the bishop for Lepore's removal. One faction broke off completely from Mount Carmel and built a beautiful chapel, San Rocco, at West 36th Avenue and Osage, one block away. They were led by Frank Damascio, architect and principal donor of the chapel, and one of the wealthiest Italians in the city.

It was now 1902. The bishop refused to bless San Rocco and the members considered becoming a part of the Greek Orthodox Church. Matters went along uneasily for some months, brightened only by the appearance of a quiet dark-eyed little nun from Chicago who came to Denver in 1902. She found what was described as a pitiable condition existing among some of the boys and girls of the poorer Italian families, who, because of bilingual difficulties, were growing up without religious training. She also found a number of orphans. She lost no time in establishing the Mount Carmel parish school and served as a teacher. On the third floor of a convent which she established for her order of Missionary Sisters of the Sacred Heart she founded a small orphanage and walked the streets of North Denver, begging for beds, bedding, and food. Her name was Mother Francis Xavier Cabrini who, in 1946, became the first American citizen to be sanctified by the Roman Catholic Church.

November 20, 1903 the struggles between the factions of the North Denver Italian churches came to a startling climax. Father Lepore, then about 35 years old, was found lying in a pool of blood in the doorway between the rectory and sanctuary, several bullets in his body. A young man from the same home town in Italy, who had recently arrived in Denver from Pittsburgh, was a few feet away, also felled by a bullet. Neither was dead. Giuseppe Service, the young man, was assumed by police to be the assailant; however, no murder weapon was ever found; and he answered every question with a shrug and "I don't know." Both men died the next morning, and the mystery of the murders has never been solved.

The Mount Carmel Italian Church building of red and cream colored brick (not the sandstone and marble of which Lepore had dreamed) was completed by the Servite pastor who was put in charge. The church was dedicated in 1904, although it had only the four walls

Mount Carmel Italian Church
(Our Lady of Mount Carmel)

and a canvas roof. The church has continued under the Servite Fathers, an order founded in Italy.

San Rocco Chapel was used for a time by a few of St. Patrick's parish, since Bishop Matz had suspended Father Carrigan from his priestly duties and said that couples married by him would not be considered wed. Later the San Rocco building was used by Mount Carmel for a parochial school, until it was razed in 1955.

The Italians at last had their own church and their own festivals, especially the Feast of San Rocco, celebrated each year to the present with music, a parade about the streets of North Denver, with men vying for the honor of carrying the statue of their patron saint, a typical Italian village celebration.

That sector of North Denver really was an Italian village, a Little Italy. Presenting a united front against the prejudices of the Anglos, the Irish, the Germans, they clung to old country ways. They had laughter and music — and hard work. The women baked their luscious loaves of bread in outside globular ovens, and they roamed the many vacant lots picking succulent dandelion leaves for salads. The men who had come from the agricultural south of Italy tended their vegetable gardens in the Platte River bottoms or on the many undeveloped areas of the city. Long before sunrise their wagons were loaded with produce to be taken to the City Market on Cherry Creek.

Some of the men were gardeners on the big estates about the city. Others drove the streets, bright colored fruits and vegetables in their wagons, buckets dangling beneath, perhaps a straw hat on the horse and a faded umbrella over the wagon seat. In those days of poor refrigeration, housewives learned to wait to buy fresh fruits and vegetables until they heard the melodious accented call of "String beans, fresh corn, water-melones, fresh can-ta-lopes."

Some of the men from the northern provinces, better educated, more adaptable, lived scattered about the city, and many became wealthy and prominent. Some were skilled laborers, working the booming building trade, carving the sandstone and marble decorations so popular on the houses of those turn-of-the-century years; others made intricately carved cemetery monuments. Some became doctors, lawyers, merchants. Others, well trained in music, were soon hired for entertainment about the city, either individually or in bands.

There were those who started their own businesses, often in the imported food or liquor business. (How else could their countrymen buy olive oil, garlic, parmesan or ricotta cheese, oregano — products which the Anglo housewives shunned?)' Some Italians became chefs at fine restaurants, others owned restaurants, grocery stores, mercantile companies. These more skilled, better educated, or ambitious men usually took out American citizenship papers as soon as they could. At that time wives automatically became citizens when their husbands did.

One of these men, Frank Damascio, the donor and architect of San Rocco Chapel, was one of the leading builders in the city, and was prominent in the erection of such structures as the Brown Palace Hotel, the Mining Exchange Building, and the Cathedral of the Immaculate Conception. Mr. Damascio, with his tiny wife, had come originally to Trinidad, Colorado, later moving to Denver. He was a small man with a huge walrus mustache, a talented man who drew most of his own architectural plans, and an amateur sculptor who enjoyed making humorous pieces, such as a statue of one of his favorite dogs, or a pair called Mutt and Jeff, after the comic strip characters.

Mr. Damascio died in 1925, but his wife lived to be a hundred years old. They had three children, one of whom died in childhood. Their daughter, Elisa, did not fit the mold of the submissive, domestic Italian housewife. While still a girl, she was her father's helper, working on his blueprints with considerable skill. She studied nursing and, after her marriage, opened a lying-in and convalescent hospital in her father's home at 3611 Osage Street, an elegant house with gray stone front, bay windows, and interior marble floors, built in 1891 and now being restored. Elisa Damascio Palladino the mother of two children, was active in politics, forsaking the traditional Democratic allegiance of the Italians to be a Republican worker. In 1935 she became Denver's first woman city council member, appointed by Mayor Begole to fill a vacancy. She also was on the first Basic Sciences committee, a state examining board which passes on the applications of doctors in various

Damascio house,
slated for demolition,
is being restored

43

medical fields to practice in Colorado. Elisa Damascio Palladino did much to help the cause of not only Italian women but Italians in general.

Many of the men who came from the industrial provinces became miners in Colorado, some in the mountains, others in the coal mines of southern Colorado and those north of Denver in such towns as Erie, Firestone, or Frederick. Trains on Saturday evenings brought them to their homes and families in North Denver, and for a few hours bright music and laughter rang through Little Italy as all its inhabitants, all hard workers, relaxed for a while.

The Italians were slow to become Americanized. They had four Italian language newspapers. Their neighbors, their priest, the nuns, most of their fellow workers all spoke Italian, so why should they learn English? They had their own societies, rather like our credit unions today, where a member paid a dollar a month and could borrow whatever was necessary for a small business, whether it be barber tools, shoe repair equipment, a vegetable wagon. The Italians were taking care of their own and warned those who might think of moving away from Little Italy that they'd not have any protection in that strange and prejudiced world outside their own tight community.

These native Europeans did not trust American banks. Saving and the business of foreign exchange, as men sent money home, were handled informally by Italian grocers. People would leave their money with the grocers, without interest, and actually without any assurance that they would get it all back. Finally state laws were enacted forbidding anyone to conduct a banking or exchange business unless he was duly authorized by the state banking commission. The Frazzini brothers, who had dealt heavily in money exchange through their mercantile business, applied for a charter for an Italian American Bank. The headquarters were at 2134-15th Street, later moved to 15th and Larimer. Prospero Frazzini was president, Cesare Frazzini vice president, Felicito Frazzini cashier. They were a small organization, showing a capital of $100,000 and a surplus of $14,000, according to an ad in *Colorado and the Italians in Colorado* (Perilli, Dr. Giovanni, 1922.) The Frazzinis were outstanding citizens of the Italian community and Prospero had been awarded by the king the highest honor ever given to an Italian living outside the boundaries of his native land. The three brothers, besides their banking and mercantile businesses, were also involved in coal mining companies as stockholders or directors.

The last of January, 1925, excited rumors ran through North Denver. The Italian American Bank had failed! Its closed doors were crowded by a gathering of anxious depositors. They did not panic, even though family savings were completely wiped out. Bitterly they received the word and possibly thought that they had been right all along not to trust bankers. But Prospero?

As facts developed, it was found that Prospero had made unsecured loans to one of the fuel companies of which he was a stockholder to meet their payroll. Final figures showed there was a shortage of over $200,000. Prospero, the leader of the community, the trusted fellow countryman, the recipient of highest honors from the crown itself, was found guilty of grand larceny and sentenced to five to eight years at the Colorado penitentiary. Prophetically, he said he would not live to serve the full term. He died of what was called a broken spirit in the penitentiary May 29, 1926, only a few months after he was sentenced.

Prohibition and bootlegging

For several years growing forces had been pushing for prohibition of alcoholic beverages in the whole nation. Backed principally by small town and rural areas, and augmented by a large Protestant bloc in both cities and towns, prohibition became a major political issue, with a Prohibition party appearing on election tickets.

Liquor control was adopted in Colorado in 1916, but the state law had many loopholes. It allowed sale of alcohol for medicinal purposes, and it was easy for anyone to find a health problem either in himself or someone in his family that could be eased by a spirituous medication. Wyoming was a "wet" state, and the hundred miles from Cheyenne to Denver were a relatively short distance to run good liquor into the city. Foreign whiskeys and wines were shipped into Texas ports and, often diluted, found their way to Colorado through well established channels. Shipments were easily camouflaged in boxes of legitimate products. The governor had been allowed by the law only $5000 to police the liquor business, hardly enough to plug all leaks. The European-oriented society elite and clubs of the city and the liquor-inured could always get alcoholic beverages. The state law obviously was not taken seriously by a large portion of the population.

National prohibition laws became effective in 1920. This eliminated medicinal alcohol in Colorado. What had been a game of eluding state prohibition agents grew like a gargantuan baby into the deadly serious business of mixing with federal authorities and of gangsterism. Criminals as well as small-time law breakers were spawned. During the depression years of 1929 to 1933 small peddlers or makers of illicit liquor often were family men caught in a financial bind who saw a chance to make some much needed money. Brash young men, who had seen their fathers work long hard hours at back-breaking work in order to support their families, were quick to see the easy money in bootlegging.

Ingenious tricks of sale were devised. Bootleggers delivered at night in high speed cars, but the illegal stuff was also carried in baby buggies or children's little red wagons. Peepholes in doors, guards lounging outside, secret knocks — all were used at bootlegging establishments and speakeasies. There were stills in mountain cabins, in city dwellings, in depressed mining communities which had been struggling for existence ever since 1893. Authorities in mountain towns and counties simply looked the other way where the making of hard liquor was concerned, especially if hush money was involved. And, of course, there were those who would brew or distill anything. They used old radiator coils from junk automobiles for equipment, and distilled everything from prunes to plain sugar syrup. The inevitable "rotgut" and wood alcohol made their appearance. Bathtub gin became a symbol of the times. It was estimated that 170 deaths occurred from bad liquor in 1922 in Denver (*Denver Post*, December 20, 1922, page 1). Amateur chemists were paid by anxious purchasers to check booze for poisonous substances. Sanitary conditions in some home stills were unbelievable, and the excuse was given that dead rats or mice gave a certain "body" to the liquor.

Since the 1880's there had been an intricately organized underworld in Denver, known as the best town in the country for con men. In addition to the elaborate confidence games, which seldom bothered with anything under $5,000, this underworld involved protection of prostitutes and pimps, and the corruption of many city officials, police, and city detectives. After prohibition was put into effect, the organization naturally became involved in bootlegging and the transportation of liquor, with big and regular payoffs to law officers.

In a dramatic move in August 1922, the district attorney of Denver rounded up 34 members of the organized underworld, stylishly dressed men who lived in fine homes and apartments on Capitol Hill or in downtown hotels. Those who did not jump bond were convicted on confidence game charges for sentences of varying lengths.

None of those arrested or convicted had Italian names. Nevertheless, the name of lawbreaker or bootlegger seemed to be attached to the whole Italian population, and Little Italy was pointed to as a center of lawlessness. Part of the blame for this can be laid to the still prevailing prejudice against the Italians. Frederick G. Bonfils, co-owner and co-editor of the *Denver Post*, with his partner, Harry H. Tammen, who dubbed their sheet "the paper with a heart and a soul," was always quick to exploit what they called "the pulse of the people," especially if it was moralistic. Bonfils, who had anything but a pure white reputation, made the most of the prejudice against Little Italy and implied in editorials that this was where all evil in Denver originated. This enraged the Italians so much that, even today, some old timers will not subscribe to the *Post*.

When the Ku Klux Klan began its rapid growth in Colorado in the 20's and 30's, the Catholic Italians were a natural target of its bigotry. The Klan had tremendous influence on many public officials. At one point Denver's chief of detectives ordered every soft drink parlor in North Denver (but not in other sections of the city) closed on the premise that each was a front for a speakeasy.

It cannot be denied that more than a few Italians were involved in bootlegging, built on what was originally an innocent foundation. When those from the winemaking provinces of their home country had found that good wine grapes could not be grown in Colorado, they banded together annually to ship carloads of grapes from

California. (This was before prohibition.) Wine had always been part of their way of life. Even little children were given a sip of wine or beer at meals. This was true of not only Italians, but of almost every other European in this country. The ones who had obtained American citizenship had been told that they were citizens of the land of the free. Why, then, had their freedom to drink wine been taken from them? What had happened to the freedom of the liquor and food importers to bring good beverages from Europe into this country?

It was a natural progression from making wine for family consumption to selling to others. Inevitably gangsterism and its attendant vices of hijacking, murders, corruption were not slow to infiltrate the business. There was rivalry between the big operators in Pueblo, Trinidad, Leadville, and Denver. There was still provincial and national distrust between the different groups and families of immigrants. The desire for power and for more money led to payoffs, bribes, and shakedowns.

Joe Carlino from Pueblo tried to become king of the liquor business in Denver and caused a crime wave which resulted in kidnappings, his brother's murder, a mysterious explosion which leveled his own Denver home, and finally Joe's own murder on a lonely road outside Pueblo.

Little Joe Roma, who had a small grocery and was involved in illegal trafficking, was riddled by bullets as he sat in his living room playing his mandolin. After he was disposed of, there was a chance for other small-time characters to get in on the big money.

The Eighteenth Amendment was repealed in 1933, marking the end of the most disastrous, most expensive effort to legislate morals our country had known. In Denver Joe Roma's murder in February of 1933 was the end of most of the violence connected with illegal liquor.

Denver settled down to other urban problems, but not without leaving a stigma on North Denver that has never been completely erased.

North Denver today

The early well-to-do who had built in North Denver, because it seemed to be an ideal location for fine estates, long ago had moved away, discouraged by the lack of a viaduct to the city and by the growth of small cottages around them. They were squeezed out, as it were. Many of the Irish moved, squeezed out they said, by the Italians. After having been a close community for many years, Little Italy began to lose its cohesiveness as younger families, Americanized, moved west into the Highlands section or into the Jefferson County suburbs of Wheat Ridge and Lakewood. Others, as they gained wealth and standing, moved to more prestigious parts of the city. They felt they were squeezed out of North Denver, as the earlier inhabitants had felt, this time by a new wave of immigrants.

These new people are unique in that they cannot be called by one general name. Some call themselves Mexicans, others Hispano, or Spanish-surnamed, or Spanish-speaking, or Spanish-Americans. A good percentage of them have come from the San Luis Valley of Colorado, and their forebears were Spanish who came directly across the southwest from New Orleans without any contact with Mexico. Their speech is more purely Castilian than is the Spanish spoken by Mexicans. Of these, some are still pure Spanish, others several generations ago mixed with the North American Indians. Those from farther south are principally Spanish mixed with earlier natives of Mexico. Others have Anglo names, either purposely Anglicized or of Spanish derivation only on the mother's side. The younger ones, often more radical, call their people Chicano.

Some are illegal aliens. Many, legally or illegally, came to northeastern Colorado to do the back-breaking work of the beet fields, and then drifted to the city. Like many of the Italians of a generation or two before, these are largely the poor and unschooled. But others are well educated and many hold positions of importance in the city.

Their community is not concentrated geographically as was the Italian neighborhood. They are scattered into all parts of the city; and those older established families of North Denver are considered the conservative ones, living their lives quietly, working hard at their jobs. In recent years the Chicanos have formed a community that is not so much geographic as cultural. They are striving for identification, dignity, and individuality in a country that has never been a melting pot but an amal-

Our Lady of Guadalupe is a newcomer to the church scene of North Denver

gam of cultures. They face the prejudice and difficulties the Italians faced a generation ago. Even though they are not newcomers, job opportunities lie in the more menial lines.

They want to build a pride and knowledge of their heritage and culture and pass it on to the children and young people. The new-found aggressiveness of some of the Chicanos has caused problems in North Denver.

Little stone house in old North Denver

There is conflict between them and the Italians who remember how hard they or their parents worked for their homes on these sites, their citizenship, and their own recognition. Some of the Chicanos want to give the name of La Raza Park to Columbus Park, at West 38th Avenue and Osage Street, for which the early Italians struggled. These people are asking for, and deserve, better recognition in community affairs, consistent zoning in their neighborhoods and rejuvenation of rundown areas.

The Spanish-surnamed residents have their own ethnic Catholic Church, Our Lady of Guadalupe, at West 36th Avenue and Kalamath, only three blocks from the Italian ethnic church. Our Lady of Guadalupe parish was started in the 1930's with a few members, but now the building, erected in 1947, of an attractive Spanish architecture, is packed at Sunday masses with members of this group of people who are trying to find a place in the whole community and still retain pride in their own heritage. Various small Protestant congregations are also scattered about the area.

From the well-to-do of the 1880's to the three waves of new settlers — Irish, Italian, Chicano, all of whom successively lived in the little cottages of North Denver, one wonders what the next step will be for this part of the city.

The rich river valley of the South Platte has been taken over by a rushing roaring eight lane highway; the truck farms have been replaced by industries which are creeping steadily over the old picturesque residential part of the city known as North Denver, or sometimes by its original name of Highland. The early business district along 15th Street, where former banks and prestige store buildings have been used as warehouses, is undergoing a rebirth as craftsmen and artists move into the rehabilitated shops.

The historic confluence of Cherry Creek with the river, so long a neglected eyesore and a disgrace to the city, has, in 1975, been converted into a park development. A white water racing course, an amphitheater, bicycle and pedestrian paths along an urban river which never freezes over — not even General William Larimer, with his penchant for starting towns, could have envisioned what would happen to the area where he stumbled across the ice of a frozen South Platte in December, 1858.

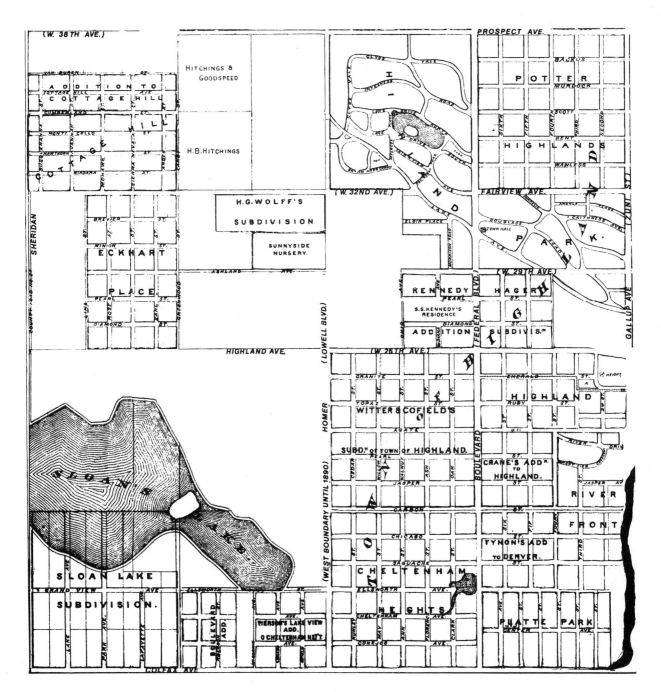

Highlands: The Elite Suburb

The beginning

Plows and drags, teams and men had been working for days filling gullies and scraping out what now appeared to be streets. Baffled citizens of North Denver stared at the interweaving serpentine streets just across Gallup Avenue (now Zuni Street) from their town and muttered, "Must be laid out on the old cowpaths — or, more'n likely, paths cowboys make going home from the saloons." The reality is that this was to be Highland Park, advertised as "the most complete and beautiful villa residence park in the United States." No money and no labor were to be spared to make it a perfect Eden.

Highland Park was organized by Dr. William A. Bell, General William J. Palmer, and others who had been active in early railroading ventures. Dr. William Bell was the president of the Highland Park Company and was named first trustee on March 4, 1875 when the company was organized in London.

Dr. Bell was born in Ireland, the son of a famous London doctor. He himself went to medical school but never got around to practicing much medicine. He was typical of the young wealthy Englishmen who came to the west for adventure and stayed to build successful ventures. He was sent by his father to a medical meeting in St. Louis in 1867, which he attended lackadaisically, but instead of returning to London to disseminate the information on homeopathic medicine which he was supposedly learning, he signed on with the builders of the Kansas Pacific railroad as a photographer, although he knew nothing of this new field of picture taking. On this surveying trip which crossed the west, Bell became a close friend of General William J. Palmer, and together, with money from wealthy friends, they built the Denver & Rio Grande Railroad, the towns of Colorado Springs and Manitou, and had their fingers in almost every business pie in the state of Colorado.

Dr. William Alexander Bell was a bubbly fun-loving individual, who also insisted on adherence to English customs at his home in Manitou, and was largely responsible for Colorado Springs' being dubbed "Little London" for many years. When he thought up the plans for his new suburb of Denver, named Highland Park, he must have been in a whimsical mood for he planned this venture on the raw windswept hills and gullies of Colorado to resemble a Scottish village. He had the 288 acres laid out on a most marvelously bewildering plat of curving streets, avenues, places, crescents, roads, and drives, all with Scottish names.

Originally Highland Park was bound on the south by Lake Avenue (later called West Lake Place and now North Speer Boulevard) which had been a 25-foot-deep gully; on the west by Homer Boulevard, now Lowell Boulevard, on the north by Prospect Avenue (now West 38th Avenue), in a roughly elliptical shape, beginning at Ashland Avenue (now West 29th) and Gallup Avenue (now Zuni) and angling northwest. In 1887 the Highland Park Company vacated its claim to the western part of this property, losing such fascinating streets as Brynn Myrr Crescent, Melrose Place, Cameron Drive, Inverness Road, but other streets such as Argyle, Clyde, Dunkeld, Caithness, Firth, Fife, and Douglas remain. The curving streets continue to some extent to West 34th and Irving Street, where old maps show a small lake.

Within this subdivision the Highland Park Hotel was started in 1875 by the Chapin Brothers at what is now West 33rd Avenue and Federal Boulevard. All Denver society put on its finest to come to the opening of this beautiful suburban hotel and the *Daily Tribune* of June 25, 1875 reported: "The site of the building is such as to command crisp invigorating fresh air and a view of more country and high mountains than any hotel in or around Denver. Every inhalation is as of an inspiration from a glass of highest champagne. . . . The hotel is superbly furnished and in the billiard room and parlors, in the corridors and office everyone found comfort and pleasure." The hotel burned after a few years and in 1884 a lake which had furnished water for the building was declared a nuisance and drained. A tree nursery was started on the property by D. S. Grimes, a long-time prominent florist in Highlands. The acreage was designated a Denver city park in 1899 and again named Highland Park. A double row of cottonwoods had encircled the block and a few remain, the same indispensable species of old prairie trees which, more than anything else, furnished landmarks, shelter and fuel to the early pioneers who traveled across the plains. Woodbury Branch Library, one of the four original branches, was built in this park in 1912.

By 1875 others, besides the "Rio Grande gentlemen" were seeing the possibilities of these lands west of North Denver, even higher than those hills that Larimer called Highland (no "s"). In 1875 the village of Highlands was incorporated. It included the development of the confusing Scottish named streets of Highland Park, but by 1890 it contained 35 other subdivision developments.

The town of Highlands' east boundary was the street separating it from North Denver, Gallup Avenue (now Zuni) to the point where it met the Platte River to the south, then followed the center of the river to Colfax Avenue, also known as the South Golden Road. Colfax Avenue became Highlands' south boundary to the west line of our present Lowell Boulevard. In 1890 this west boundary was moved to the county line between Arapahoe and Jefferson Counties, now Sheridan Boulevard. The north boundary line was the old Prospect Trail, then known as Prospect Avenue and now West 38th Avenue.

Horatio B. Bearce might well be called "Mr. Highlands." A man of meticulous appearance, tall and dignified, he was one of the earliest pioneers in the Denver area, coming here in 1859 from New England, where he was a member of a prominent Bostonian family. Like almost everyone else, he tried his hand at mining, first in Gilpin County and then in Leadville. Despite his many other interests, he never recovered from prospecting fever, although in later years he was identified by the more dignified title of mining broker. After he brought his wife and daughter from Boston, he received title, dated February 26, 1869, to eighty acres of those barren hills far northwest of Denver. The Bearce house is still standing, stuccoed and enlarged, at 2438 Federal Boulevard. There is a handsome horse chestnut tree in the front yard, undoubtedly planted by the Bearces and now more than a hundred years old.

Soon after Bearce and his family were settled, he made plans for the Town of Highlands, laying out his ranch into blocks and lots in 1871. He was the first to sign the petition for a town charter April 8, 1876, and was the town's first mayor. He had previously served on the first Board of Directors of School District #17, Arapahoe County, which covered all the northwest area around Denver, and over the next few years he held several offices on that school board.

Mr. Bearce was active in almost everything going on —Patriot Sons of America of which he was an officer, Odd Fellows, Pioneer Association, Knights of Pythias. In his early years in Highlands he was president of the Agricultural Society of Denver and of the Colorado Agricultural Fair, a member of the territorial legislature, trustee of the new agricultural college at Fort Collins, president of the Territorial Association of Colorado, a member of Colorado Board of Real Estate Agents, president of the Democratic Club, and even a judge of equestriennes at the Boulder Fair in 1870. In the 1880's he was appointed by the governor to be Major General of the Colorado militia. He also worked in the temperance movement, perhaps one reason why the town of

The house and tree
General Bearce started
over 100 years ago

Highlands was very anti-liquor. Needless to say, he was one of the most prominent men in the state.

In 1876 when the state constitutional convention had finished its work and ratification by the people was assured, plans were made for a grand celebration — and a grand celebration it was. July 4th was chosen as the date and General Horatio B. Bearce was a natural for the marshal of the whole affair. Jerome Smiley in his *History of Denver* says: "The city put on its holiday attire, invited all the people from near and far, and sent forth a street pageant that is memorable to this day." It started out with the Knights Templar, plumes flying, uniforms resplendent, mounted on coal black steeds, their officers on milky white horses. There were the best bands available, rich uniforms, the Governor's Guard, the Mitchell Grays, more bands, the Masons two by two, the Pioneers, the Odd Fellows in royal purple on white horses, the Sir Knights, a brass band from Erie, floats with flowers and pretty girls, the volunteer fire companies, the printers, an infantry division, the bakers, a long line of German turners and Scandinavians. The parade wound about the streets, ending at a grove of cottonwoods along the Platte, where the whole town picnicked and listened to speeches and more band music, and congratulated themselves again and again that they were at last members of a state of the United States. It was a great day and General Bearce could well be proud.

That same year the Bearce family moved from Highlands to a home in Denver at 367 Stout (now 15th and Stout Streets). He continued to be busy with his many interests, but it was that old persistent gold fever that brought tragedy to him.

In June, 1884 General Bearce with a business partner went to inspect a placer mine they owned near Twin Lakes, Colorado. At the toll gate at Twin Lakes a local prominent rancher accosted them. There had been some hard feelings because the mine threatened to damage the ranch property and cut off or pollute the water. Bearce had received reports that the claim had been jumped and he told Mr. Deering, the rancher, that he might be held responsible. Bearce and his partner went on to the mine, spent the day doing assessment work on it, and about six o'clock started home in a spring wagon. They were again met by Deering at the toll gate. He shouted at the General about his accusation of jumping the claim. Bearce stood up in the wagon to his full dignified height, but before he could speak, Deering pulled a brand new revolver from his pocket and shot him. General Bearce was rushed to doctors at Leadville. His wife, daughter, and friend, David H. Moffat, arrived from Denver on the first train to be with him. Bearce was conscious and gave his daughter instructions about his estate. He died the day after the shooting, and Highlands, as well as the whole state, lost one of its most admired leaders and important pioneers. There was a grand funeral in Denver, arranged by the Denver camp of the Patriotic Sons of America, which had elected him to the office of president at about the same time as the shooting.

Highlands' proud ambition

To be a perfect Eden, a Utopia, was the dream and ambition of the whole town of Highlands. The people of the town were a very proud people. They were proud of their homes, and there was to be no dirty industry in the town. The men were to earn their living in Denver and then return at night to the quiet clean atmosphere of the Highlands. They were proud of their gardens, their trees, their churches, their schools, their pure air, their pure water, their pure morals — especially their pure morals.

Morals and laws

Highlands had a $5,000 annual liquor license fee so, of course, there were no saloons. They did not permit gambling, prostitution, or "houses of ill fame." This was at a time when Denver was wide open and its red light district was known from coast to coast.

Highlands had an ordinance against playing marbles or flying kites in streets or alleys, despite the fact that traffic was limited to an occasional buggy or delivery wagon. They decreed that "no person shall drive, toss, knock or play ball, marbles, pitch pennies, quoits or fly any kites on any street, alley or highway within the limits of the town of Highlands" (*Highlands Ordinances*, 1889). They had an ordinance against quarreling or fighting, and against using any common, vulgar, indecent, abusive, foul, or improper language.

Pure water

Highlanders had a number of different sources of water. Early Highlands residents dug wells for domestic use, but irrigation water was of prime importance for the building of a permanent settlement.

An article in the *Denver Tribune* of May 28, 1874 read: "The cactus, soaproot, lizard and rattlesnake have held undisputed sway in this hot parched sand for ages past, and until a few years ago the land was considered worthless. But water is everything and money, with labor and science, can accomplish almost anything. . . . Water in abundance from the Table Mountain ditch has been brought along the highest hills and trained to run in countless ditches all over the [Highlands] Park, and vegetation is made to grow where vegetation has heretofore been almost unknown." Backers planned a series of lakes, to be landscaped with artificial islands, beautiful groves, and fountains.

This elaborately dreamed system originated with Hiram G. Wolff, an early settler in Highlands, who had a farm and tree nursery between what are now Lowell and Newton, West 29th and West 30th Avenues. Mr. Wolff, helped by hired hands, had dug the original ditch with his own "fresno," a deep scoop drawn by a horse or team. His ditch, known as the Highland Ditch, in 1882 became part of the Rocky Mountain Ditch system. It is interesting that rights to this ditch system remained with the Wolff family until 1970 when they were sold to the Coors Brewery Company of Golden.

The reservoirs of the system were what are now Rocky Mountain Lake, which had been a small watering hole, Berkeley Lake, and Lake Rhoda in Lakeside Amusement Park, which had been named West Berkeley Lake. Sloan's Lake was also part of the system, but the story of Sloan's Lake is given in much more detail farther along in this book. Various small reservoirs, either private or belonging to water companies, were scattered about the new little town of Highlands.

Early in the 1880's an amazing source of water was found — artesian water, bursting to be released. The first artesian well was struck by an R. L. McCormick who was boring for coal near West 17th and Federal. The water spurted 100 feet into the air and McCormick was unhappy; he wanted coal, not water. By 1886 there were over 130 artesian wells in the Denver area. Many downtown stores, hotels, and office buildings had their own wells, which furnished water much superior to that the city of Denver was drawing from the Platte River. But it remained for a group of men in Highlands to form an artesian water company, the only such company in the United States at the time.

It was named the Beaver Brook Water Company, organized in 1886. The company's original plan was to bring water from Beaver Brook, a tributary of Clear Creek on the west side of Lookout Mountain, an ambitious project which did not succeed. They changed their source to artesian water and had four primary wells, one at the northeast corner of "the Boulevard" and Lake Avenue (now Federal and North Speer), another at the southeast corner of what is now West 32nd Avenue and Lowell Boulevard, two in the block bounded by (now) West 34th and 35th Avenues, Alcott and Zuni Streets, where the rhythmic beat of the pumps was assurance that there was water in the pipes. The company had about 15,000 taps serving customers east of Lowell in Highlands and also some in North Denver. This was at a time when Denverites had sieves on their faucets to catch the small fish that came through from the Platte.

The Arbuckle Building, built around 1884, at the site of the main well at the northeast corner of Federal and Speer, originally was the clubhouse of the Highland Park development. It was an attractive stone building with a wide verandah on two sides. The first floor housed city offices, a volunteer hose company, and Highland Park offices. When the water company moved their offices into the building in 1890, they added a small electrical generating plant and a water bottling room. On the second floor were social rooms and a large hall which was used at various times for dances, dancing school, gym classes, high school graduation, lodge and church organization meetings. When a nearby elementary school had to place classes about the neighborhood, some were held in these Arbuckle Building rooms, and one man who attended fourth grade there commented, "The rooms were heated by fireplaces and we always hoped for a windy day when the room would fill with smoke and class would be dismissed."

The president of the Beaver Brook Water Company was Frank P. Arbuckle, whose home was a three story

Arbuckle Building, with tall tank over large artesian well

frame house at West 33rd and Bryant Street, built in 1885, one of the few large frame buildings now standing in the area. Arbuckle was one of the most prominent men in the state. He was interested in several water companies, in mining, investments, and politics. He was chairman of the State Central Committee of the Democratic party. In November, 1896, when Arbuckle was 44 years old, he went to New York City on business. He was a hearty, convivial person, and one evening while in New York he went to a saloon and there bought drinks for the house, displaying a large bankroll. Gradually some well dressed but unsavory characters attached themselves to him, took him from bar to bar, everyone becoming more inebriated during the evening. At last Arbuckle left to return to his hotel alone, but at three o'clock the next morning his body was found in a vacant lot. His diamond stickpin, gold watch and chain, pearl gray overcoat, and of course the bankroll were all missing.

The Arbuckle Building remained long after Arbuckle was gone. The water company underwent many changes in management. The whole picture of water interests in the Denver area, companies dissolved or acquired by other companies, court battles, bankruptcies, was complex and confused. Not all homes in Highlands were served by the artesian water company, not all relied on

Frank Arbuckle built one of the few large frame houses in Highlands

Oakes Home, second tubercular home in country

only one source. Some residents had artesian wells in their own yards and piped this into their homes and to some neighbors. Some people, especially in the more lightly settled areas, relied on ditch water for irrigating their lawns and gardens and bought spring water from tank wagons which made the rounds of the neighborhood. The town of Highlands owned the Beaver Brook Water Company at one time, and sometime along the way it became the Highlands Water Company (or, as it is listed in the city directories, the Denver Highlands Water Company). This later company had a much diminished supply, for the water table was lower, and they

served possibly 500 taps. At last the company, still housed in the Arbuckle Building, was sold with its properties to the Denver Union Water Company around 1917. The wells were capped, and the building was converted into apartments. It burned about 1950.

Pure air

Highlanders were very proud of the town's pure air. Denver's air by this time was polluted by smoke which drifted south in the river valley from three smelters, Argo, Grant, and Globe. Highlanders bragged that their

Hallie Bond

Beautiful entrance to St. Elizabeth's Retreat, formerly Oakes Home (now razed)

city was "situated upon a high eminence, proudly over-looking her smoky neighbor, the city of Denver, her [Highlands] atmosphere untarnished by smelter or factory smoke, but as pure and fresh and sweet as the God of nature ever gave to man."

Tuberculosis at that time was the No. 1 killer in the country, and the crystalline dry air of Highlands seemed miraculous to the thousands who flocked to Colorado, since unpolluted dry air, rest, and good food constituted the only known cure or help. Some sufferers were brought to Colorado on stretchers, completely ravaged and destined to die here thousands of miles from their homes. Others, also brought on stretchers, lived to their eighties and became some of the well known leaders in Colorado's expanding business and politics.

People came with incipient cases, rested a year or two, and had arrested cases for the rest of their long lives. Every family in Highlands, it seemed, had a relative or close friend with the disease and many homes had open sleeping porches for them, or little tent houses in their backyards. These were structures with wooden floors and walls to about four vertical feet, with canvas upper walls and roofs. The tubercular person lived in these outdoor dwellings winter and summer, breathing in the miraculous air, to conquer the feared disease. There were colonies of the little tent houses, some of which became sanitariums for later scourges.

While there were many sanitariums in Highlands, the largest was Oakes Home, at West 32nd and Eliot Street, founded in 1894 by the Reverend Mr. Frederick W. Oakes of the Episcopal Diocese. It was the second tubercular home in the United States. The Reverend Mr. Oakes did not consider it a sanitarium or hospital (although it did have a hospital wing) but a "home in the most personalized sense for those seeking a return to health." There were twenty-five handsome Classic Revival buildings in the home complex, financed by donations and endowments. In 1934 the Reverend Mr. Oakes retired and the home was closed. It had treated at least 20,000 patients during the forty years it was open.

After various attempts to operate the institution for those suffering from other chronic illnesses, it was again closed in 1941 and there was talk of demolishing it, or of turning it over to the government for needed housing during World War II. Finally in 1943 the Little Sisters of the Poor purchased it for a convent. Later the Sisters of St. Francis of Colorado Springs opened it as St. Elizabeth's Retreat, a home for elderly people.

In 1974 the Sisters of St. Francis found that they must make drastic changes in the old Oakes Home buildings, in order to continue their operations as a residential home for the elderly. The beautiful 1890's structures, even though spacious, did not conform to modern regulations governing such homes. With regret they tore out the lawn and tall evergreens in front of the chapel and

home, and the charming row of residences along Decatur Street which had long been called Chapel Lane. The fine but outdated main building, with its exquisite fan shape entrance, dominated by Corinthian columns, has been replaced by modern fireproof apartment buildings. The beautiful little chapel, known as the Chapel of our Merciful Savior during the Episcopal days, and where the Reverend Mr. Oakes served as rector during his many years as superintendent of the home, has been saved and named a landmark by the City of Denver. Its name had previously been given to the former All Saints Church in North Denver, along with the pulpits, baptismal font, altars and fine wooden statues. The building is renamed Christ the King Chapel. Its brick interior, fish scale leaded windows, and classic exterior make it one of the most charming religious edifices in the city.

Other churches

Since Highlanders were a very moral, God-fearing people, there were many churches, of all denominations, in Highlands. There were also a number of parochial or church-supported institutions. Each of these has a long and interesting history of its own, which certainly cannot be covered adequately in this book; therefore, except for occasional mention, their histories have not been given. Some of the church organizations have been disbanded, but most remain, usually with new edifices at or near the original location. A few have moved from North Denver (Highland) to Highlands. Some have changed their names. Some have moved to the suburbs. New congregations have also been formed.

Public schools in Highlands

The elation of the developers at the increases in population in North Denver and Highlands was not shared by the members of the school board. They were desperate. The little one-room frame building at 15th and Central, built in 1872, was too small before the last nail was pounded into the walls. The school board tried for a couple of years to persuade the residents to accept a $15,000 bond issue. When they finally agreed to saddle themselves with such a debt, the first Ashland School was built on land given by the Highland Park Company, on Ashland Avenue (now West 29th Avenue) between

One of the most
charming religious edifices
in the city, on the grounds
of St. Elizabeth's Retreat

61

When the high school was added to the Ashland building, it was already crowded, and some classes were being placed in nearby stores. This situation was relieved temporarily by the building of the Bryant School, mentioned in Section I, and of Boulevard School in 1883. It was named for the street on which it faced, now Federal Boulevard, and located between (now) West 23rd and 24th Avenues. Boulevard was a charming two story building, but small, and additions were made in 1891 and 1904. Finally, in 1962 the first two sections were demolished, and the additions of 1904 are still being used.

By 1886 it was imperative that something be done about the Ashland building. The property had been given to the schools by the Highland Park Company "to be used for school purposes forever;" therefore, classes

The first Ashland Elementary School, 1874

Gallup Avenue (Zuni) and Firth Court. It was a handsome building for the times, built of brick and two stories high. It opened for classes in 1874. The board members were criticized for erecting a school that, in size, looked too far into the future. In 1883 the North Side High School was organized to meet on the second floor of this building. One grade at a time was added as the high school pupils progressed. The course was three years in length. The freshman class of 1883 started with fifteen pupils, but, when they graduated in 1886, the class had been reduced to six bright girls with a grade average of over 98%. High school tuition was $12 a month.

Boulevard School, built in 1883

The imposing combined Ashland Elementary and North Side High School, built in 1888

were spread out over the neighborhood again, and the first Ashland School was demolished. It was replaced by a very striking building, designed by William Quayle, one of the prominent architects of the day and a resident of Highlands. Red brick was used, trimmed lavishly with red sandstone, cut in such a way that it did not flake or weather as did so many of the sandstone trims used at that time. The triple doorway was framed by columns topped with carved capitals. The large center hall had an open stairway guarded by a graceful curved rail.

The beautiful stairway at Ashland School

Jerome Smiley, in his *History of Denver*, calls it a building of perfect appointments.

Highlands continued to grow. The annexation of the area west of Lowell Boulevard in 1890 brought a demand for a school there, and Edison Elementary School was built on Eighteenth Street (now Quitman), between Dawson and Blaine (now West 30th and 32nd Avenues). The building, first occupied in 1892, originally consisted of four rooms and basement. It was of stone and brick with an imposing cupola in the center front. In 1900 a five room wing was added on the south, and in 1902 another addition was built on the north. Nevertheless, about 1925 this building was used as an example of overcrowding in the campaigning by the school board (now District #1, City and County of Denver) for a new bond issue. The bonds passed, and a new Edison was erected on Quitman Street between West 33rd and 35th Avenues. The old Edison was demolished and the property sold, in favor of the very attractive red brick with terra cotta trim "new Edison." This, also, has had an addition, built in 1950.

Meantime, Ashland Elementary and North High School, in the same building, were again pushing out the bricks by their growth, and classes were held in the Arbuckle Building at Federal and North Speer. A large addition, almost as big as the original structure, was constructed in 1894 at the north side of Ashland. At the dedication of this section, Dr. William Smedley, who was president of the school board, said, "We have made ample provision for the high school for many years to come and at the same time have secured for the grammar grades the full capacity of an 8-room building under the same additional roof and upon ground already owned by the district."

Very good . . . except, of course, the population didn't stand still. Fifteen years later a new separate high school had to be built at West Lake Place and Ross Court (now North Speer and Eliot Street). It is a distinguished building, three stories high plus basements, of light brick with sandstone trim. The style of architecture is rather indeterminate, perhaps Renaissance, perhaps Romanesque, but the effect is noble. Two additions have been made; one, of architecture to match the main building, to be used for manual training shops; the other, built in 1959, to house a swimming pool, gym-

The first Edison School, 1892-1925

The "new" Edison,
built in 1925

Present North High School, built in 1911

nasiums, and classrooms. Many illustrious people have attended or graduated from North High, which receives its pupils from all Northwest Denver. There have been governors, doctors, lawyers, judges, actors, ministers, musicians, journalists, architects, writers, artists, educators, presidents of colleges, banks, and other busi-

nesses, and even the prime minister of a foreign country, for Golda Mabovitch Meir, prime minister of Israel from 1969 to 1974, attended North from February, 1913, to June, 1914.

Two other elementary schools in Highlands were just north of the town's south boundary. Cheltenham, at

Cheltenham School, at the edge of Highlands

Colfax and what became Irving Street, was built in 1891 in a development called Cheltenham Heights. Glen Park School, replaced by Colfax School in 1920, was a little one room (plus cloakroom) brick building at Colfax and Tennyson. It served the small affluent neighborhood on Stuart and also the children of the scattered farms and houses of the area of Highlands south of Sloan's Lake. Both Cheltenham and Glen Park were in Arapahoe County District #21.

After the high school was removed, the Ashland building continued to be used as an elementary school until 1975 when, almost ninety years old and still with

Glen Park School was replaced by Colfax School

the beautiful outside structure and inside details, but probably not suited to present school requirements, it was razed, to the futile outcries of preservationists, who felt it could be used for some other purpose. A new one-story building was erected on these grounds given by the Highland Park Company so many years ago, named the José Valdez School, in honor of a Medal of Honor winner from New Mexico.

One of the most beautiful school buildings in Denver is Lake Junior High School, built in 1926, which looks across Sloan's Lake toward the mountains. It was de-signed by Burnham Hoyt, a nationally prominent architect, whose boyhood home was in Highlands and who, with his brother Merrill, studied under Franklin Kidder, well known architect of churches in Denver in the 80's and 90's. The architecture of Lake is Tudor with a touch of Moslem influence in minaret-type domes, and looks like a medieval castle. The landscaping, with specimen trees and bushes and crannied walls, was planned by M. Walter Pesman, an outstanding land-scape architect.

The last elementary school in the old Highlands area

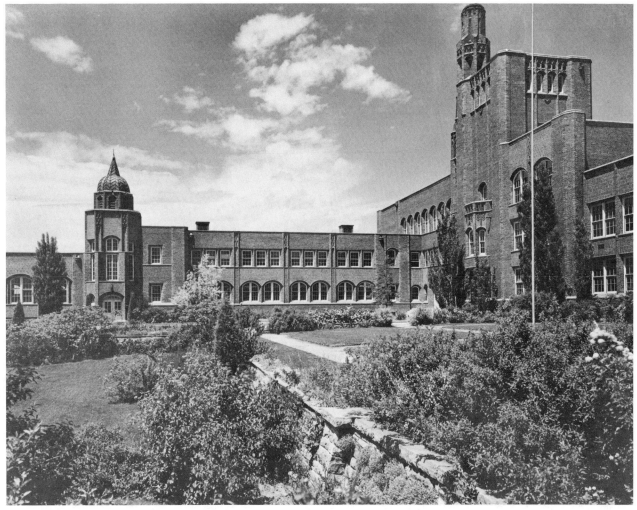

Lake Junior High School, overlooking Sloan's Lake

was necessitated by the baby boom which followed World War II. The Edward L. Brown School was erected at West 26th Avenue and Lowell Boulevard in 1952. This neighborhood, east of Sloan's Lake, was one of the last in Highlands to be developed, with most of the houses built in the 1940's.

What was school life like in the early years? Curriculum has changed so drastically that it is impossible to record it in anything but voluminous educational tomes. The boys and girls, however, have not changed very much. There were the studious ones, the restless ones, the aggressive, the quiet. Little girls had to try to be

Edward L. Brown School

ladies in their high button shoes, belted full blouses and starched skirts, and gymnastic uniforms of full below-the-knee bloomers and middy blouses. Long black stockings were the rule for boys as well as girls, and the boys wore knee-length knickers until they were in high school. So far as behavior was concerned, there were boys who slipped out to a nearby grove for a forbidden cigarette, although they were almost always caught. There were pupils who defied teachers, harassed substitutes, loved or hated their instructors and principals, usually according to the amount of love or hate the teacher or principal herself or himself inspired. Punishment was more severe in the earlier years. A principal at one of the elementary schools lashed some boys with a rubber hose while the custodian held them, because they had shot spitballs onto the ceiling of a room while they had a substitute teacher. But most principals believed in ruling with a firm but understanding discipline, augmented by a paddle hanging in the office. After School District No. 1, of the City and County of Denver, was organized in 1902, city-wide supervisors visited all the schools, and memories of certain supervisors will always linger; such as little Wilberforce Whiteman, with his meticulous thin white mustache, who was supervisor of music, and strict Jacob Schmitt, supervisor of physical education, who made the rounds to put the pupils through their calisthentics with dumbbells, Indian clubs, and wands, while he counted "Vun, doo, dree, vor." Elementary schools, before the advent of junior high schools, taught woodworking, sometimes called sloyd, to the boys, and domestic science (cooking and sewing) to the girls.

The buildings had much in common besides boys, girls, books, and teachers. All of them were heated by coal furnaces, and on cold mornings the custodians had to start feeding their fires about two-thirty, in order that the rooms would be comfortable by the time teachers and pupils arrived. The fuel usually had to be delivered during the fall months, since the coal wagons would bog down in mud or snow during the winter. This meant at least 150 tons of coal stored in every available spot in the basement. The lavatories were outside, or had outside entrances if they were attached to the building, and lines of children shivered in the cold waiting their turns. Custodians lived on the premises, either in a basement apartment or a house on the grounds. Their presence discouraged vandalism — although on one Hallowe'en a group of boys managed, at one school, to slip a cow into the main hall.

Dear in the memory of students of previous years are the school stores, one usually across the street from each school, where children could buy tablets, pencils, notebooks, and, of course, candy, gum, and cookies and other things which were goodies to them, junk to the school authorities. Finally, all school stores were discouraged or bought out by the higher-ups, so that there would be no more noontime excursions across the street.

Some of the People, their homes, gardens and trees

In 1873 when Isabella Bird (*A Lady's Life in the Rocky Mountains*, new edition copyright 1960 by the University of Oklahoma Press) went through Denver, she described it as "a great braggart city spread out, brown and treeless, upon the brown and treeless plain, which seemed to nourish nothing but wormwood and the Spanish bayonet." Of Colorado Springs she said, "To me no place could be more unattractive, from its utter treelessness."

Isabella Bird saw Denver at the end of October instead of in the spring when, if there were no late frost, she would have found the brown plains and hills dotted with white waxy sand lilies, yellow johnny-jump-ups, wild roses and golden banner on the slopes of the gullies, and the Spanish bayonet holding its flowered candles aloft. Nevertheless, Highlands could have merited the same late fall description, but its founders were determined it would not continue in this way. Highlands' landscaping was started early. In 1875, the year the town was incorporated, the city fathers gave free water for irrigation of new plantings, and 5000 shade trees were set out. Soon large estates were being built with extensive gardens, and a proud statement was printed in the *Denver Republican* January 1, 1890:

> A prettier site for a beautiful city would be hard to find. During the spring, summer and autumn months, with its tasty residences, its trees, its fruits, its lawns and flowers and shady groves, Highlands is truly a fairy-like portion of the Queen City. The Hanging Gardens of Babylon have come down through the history of the centuries as one of the marvelously constructed paradises of the world. And yet, in the 19th century of this era here in Highlands are not only four acres but 4000 acres elevated by the forces of nature above the surrounding region, affording magnificent views and scenery eclipsing any other equal area of the globe. Four thousand acres beautified by the hand and industry of man, a veritable Arcadia where happy homes are presided over by lovely queens, more refined and queenly than the one transferred from Medea to the level plains of Babylon.

Stripped of its rococo language, it still comes out that Highlands was a very good place to live. The wealthy, as

Thomas Ward home

well as the hard-working middle class who wanted the best they could possibly manage for their families, came to Highlands.

Those curving Scotch streets of Highland Park encompassed a town within a town, where the Anglo and German residents knew each other as if they were all first cousins. There were doctors, lawyers, plumbers, pharmacists, grocers. All the children went to the same schools, Ashland Elementary and North Side High School, which were in the same building. While they may have attended different Sunday Schools and churches, they all played together in the broad tree shaded lawns, and all drank lemonade together on the large enclosed back porches. Some of them grew up to follow their fathers' professions, some became Rhodes scholars at Oxford, presidents of universities, judges, politicians, bank presidents, artists, doctors, lawyers, merchants, craftsmen.

On the north edge of the subdivision of Highland Park, at 2564 West 32nd Avenue, is a brick two story home with an austere facade, now painted white with blue trim, where the warmth of love of art and literature overflowed into the town that was just emerging from its frontier roughness. This was the home of a former Missouri farmer, Thomas Ward, who brought his wife and family to Colorado around 1880 — because — as with so many of the area's pioneers — he feared his wife had tuberculosis. They raised a family of five sons and two daughters, all of whom became successful in their fields of engineering, the clergy, law, and the military service. The two daughters became artists, encouraged by the whole family. Margaret was an art teacher at North High School and later at the exclusive Wolff Hall and Wolcott School. Elsie became a nationally famous sculptor, a vital assistant to Augustus Saint-Gaudens, probably the leading late 19th century American sculptor. Elsie Ward Hering's pieces remain on view, some in private Eastern gardens; one, The Boy and a Frog, in the Denver Botanic Gardens; and a baptismal font in the Chapel of Our Merciful Savior, formerly the All Saints Episcopal Church (see page 35), where she was confirmed and married. In addition, a strong Ward influence is felt today through the personality and talent of Louisa Ward Arps, Denver author and historian, granddaughter of the first Thomas Ward. Mrs. Arps describes her grandfather's house as having a room only for his books and that the living room also was lined with bookcases. In addition, the first floor accommodated a dining room and a large kitchen, and "the toilet was on the back porch."

John W. Prout, born in Pennsylvania, son of a Welsh family, came to Colorado because of the mining possibilities. Working as a mining consultant, he traveled all over the west and into foreign countries. He owned all the houses across from the Wards, on the north side of the block between Alcott and Bryant on West 32nd Avenue, large "Denver square" homes, whose unim-

Lines of the Fisher carriage house matched the residence

aginative exteriors conceal the size and number of rooms and beauty of the interior. His own house had a fascinating finished basement with large harness room, another spacious room used as a shop where he worked on numerous inventions, a wine cellar, a fruit cellar, and a couple of large utility rooms.

Just around the corner, at 3225 Bryant Street, is a large red brick home and carriage house with matching turrets. This was the residence of the James A. Fisher family. Mr. Fisher had a thriving tent and awning business, later purchased by the Colorado Tent and Awning Company. The house, built in 1892, has beautiful carved oak woodwork and frescoed ceilings. In the yard, which was surrounded by brick and wrought iron fences, peacocks strutted. The carriage house where he kept his

The elaborate James W. Fisher residence

strikingly matched glossy black horses was quite large. Liveried footmen handled the Fisher carriages. The particular block where the Fisher home is located had a unique feature not necessary today. The block, which was surrounded on all four sides with homes, had a "turning around area" in the inside of the block, so that horses and carriages, which did not go into reverse easily, could be driven through the stable, turned around and brought back. Some of the other large homes in Highlands had sweeping driveways so that the vehicles could be driven in one end and out the other.

A brick two story house at 3132 Federal Boulevard, at

The home of Justice Benjamin C. Hilliard

the west edge of the subdivision of Highland Park, built in 1893, had been a farmhouse for a property which included one of the many orchards in Highlands. The house, in 1906, became the home of a colorful attorney, politician, and public servant. Judge Benjamin C. Hilliard came to Colorado in 1893, and was the final city attorney for the city of Highlands before annexation. He served as a state legislator around 1900, was a congressman from Colorado from 1915 to 1919, and served on the Colorado Supreme Court from 1930 to his death in August, 1951, having two terms as Chief Justice. Judge Hilliard, a warm, friendly man, had flowing silver

Ochiltree Building, first home of Central Bank & Trust

hair worn to his collar at a time when short hair was the style, and always wore a black string tie, all of which set him apart from other men, just as he was set apart by his dedication to law. His son, Benjamin C. Hilliard, Jr., was also an attorney, served in World War I, and was national head of the 40 and 8 group of the American Legion. At the time of his death in 1969, he was chief referee in bankruptcy in Denver. Judge and Mrs. Hilliard also had two daughters and an older son who became an attorney in Nevada. The house is still in the Hilliard family hands.

The east side of Highland Park, along Gallup Avenue (now Zuni) was a business district. The cable car barns were there, on the west side at West 30th Avenue. Store buildings clustered around the intersection of Fairview (32nd) and Gallup, with the Weir Building on the northwest corner, a four story building which housed stores and offices, an early movie theater, and on the top floor the Weir Hall, a popular place for meetings and dances.

At the corner of Gallup and Dunkeld Place was the Ochiltree Building, which originally was the North Side

Savings Bank, started in 1892 by Willis M. and Robert M. Marshall, brothers. The bank weathered the Panic of 1893 and moved downtown in 1896, changing its name to the Central Savings Bank, now the Central Bank and Trust Company, one of Denver's top five commercial banks at present. (A later North Denver Bank was near the same location, West Lake Place and Zuni, in the 1920's, but there is no connection.)

North of the 1890's bank at Dunkeld and Zuni (Gallup) there was a small reading room, sponsored by the Women's Christian Temperance Union, directly across Gallup Avenue, the dividing line between dry Highlands and wet North Denver, from a popular saloon. A few years later the city of Denver backed a reading room in this neighborhood, a forerunner of a public library. After Highlands was annexed to Denver, the post office occupied a large room on the street level of the Ochiltree Building. It later moved to West 32nd and Bryant, and still later to 3125 Federal.

An early business section grew up around (present) West 25th Avenue and Eliot Street, which was the end of a horse car line which met the cable cars at Colfax and Federal and traveled north on Federal to 25th. At this intersection various businesses operated: a large dry goods store, a German bakery which turned out delectable confections, a very early theater, a plumbing shop, a boarding house nearby, and at West 25th and Decatur the first Highlands city hall, in a store front building now converted to a residence, the same building in which St. Dominic's Catholic Church held its first mass.

Federal Boulevard was known officially and unofficially for all the early years as "the Boulevard," the elite street of Highlands. When the streets were alphabetized about 1904 it became Boulevard F, and it was not until 1912 that it became Federal Boulevard.

Boulevard was divided by a center row of cottonwoods for many blocks. It was a leisurely pleasant street of homes, churches, and the large city hall, and it conjures up a picture of gracious upright living. Sunday was the day for families to stroll its sidewalks, or drive down the shady street in buggies or carriages, attending church in the morning, "calling" in the afternoon.

Many of the fine homes of Highlands either faced upon the Boulevard or were clustered nearby. They were typical Victorian houses, two or three stories high, built

Stained glass window and hand-turned spindles

of stone or brick. The sidewalks and the walls surrounding the grounds were usually of sandstone. Many of the residences had turrets at the corner. Every house had stained glass windows; almost without exception the stairway landing window would be of leaded stained glass, usually a hall window and upper pane of the large front window would follow suit. Sometimes these windows were in soft pastels, sometimes in rich deep tones, geometric or stylized vines and flowers. One house has etched glass with carved graceful birds, all of colorless glass; another has a patchwork design around a glass swirl in the staircase window, the double front doors and transom above, of brilliant color. Another house has large windows of small leaded panes with only a touch of color. Woodwork in most of the houses was of fine hard

Two wrought iron fences

woods, each room of a different wood, often to match the furniture, so that there might be a cherry wood, walnut, or birdseye maple room. Some were panelled in highly polished woods, some panelling was carved. Mantels were elaborate.

Gardens with deciduous as well as evergreen trees were important, with familiar snowball bushes and lilacs filling the corners, perhaps a round bed of bright red cannas in the center, and often some lawn statuary — deer or tigers or mythological figures — to accent a spot or act as pedestal for sundial or bird bath. Wrought iron fences were the style, some of the familiar spear design, others of more unusual pattern. The spear design seemed to be the most popular because it discouraged boys from climbing or walking the fences.

No doubt the best known of all the large homes was the Woodbury mansion at West 25th and Alcott Street, a magnificent red brick and sandstone L-shaped house built for Brigadier General Roger W. Woodbury, who had come to the Denver area in 1866, one of the many Civil War veterans who came west for a new start in a new land. He had served meritoriously in the war as a captain and had been wounded. He was made a brigadier general in the Colorado National Guard. Like so many of the men of that time, he was active in almost everything going on in the new territory — newspapers, banking, railroading, mining. He was a legislator, regent of the University of Colorado, the first president of the Denver Chamber of Commerce. As one of the founders of the public library, he induced Andrew Carnegie to make a substantial gift which made the Denver library possible. (A branch library in Highlands is named for General Woodbury.) A handsome dashing man, he made and lost three fortunes — in mining, agriculture, and publishing.

In 1885 General Woodbury built his palatial home on a hill overlooking the Platte River valley and the town of Denver. The house had gold plated and sterling silver doorknobs, carved hardware, Tiffany stained glass windows (one cost $3500 at that time), crystal chandeliers. Rooms were paneled in hand carved imported woods. There were pure gold accents on the tile fireplaces. The music room walls were covered with lavender satin. The bathroom's elaborate fittings were gold-plated.

In the Panic of 1893 General Woodbury lost his

General Roger W. Woodbury's palatial home

lovely home, although statements have been made that he had never stepped inside it after his wife, for whom he built it, died. He himself died in 1903.

The house suffered degradation, first being made into apartments, then bought by interests who left it empty. It was vandalized by maliciousness and by the acquisitiveness of antique hunters. With every window broken, the trees and bushes dead from neglect, the sandstone wall surrounding the estate crumbling, the house was finally razed in 1958. A handsome modern office complex has been erected on the block. The street, Woodbury Court, was closed and the site renamed Diamond Hill. (The builders selected the name from Diamond Avenue, which became West 27th Avenue, a block away.) About all that remain as symbols of General Woodbury's generosity and public spirit are the Florentine Renaissance Woodbury Branch Library at West

33rd Avenue and Federal and a building on the campus of the University of Colorado.

Another stately home, now replaced by a small apartment house, was built by Silas S. Kennedy at the northwest corner of what is West 27th Avenue and Federal. Kennedy, born in Indiana in 1837, came to Colorado in 1860 with Horace Greeley to found the Union Colony, and was active in the milling business there. He owned three productive mines at Gregory Gulch, Jimtown, and Lake City.

In 1880 Kennedy moved to Highlands and had a farm of some nine city blocks, with a frame farmhouse at (now) 2727 Grove Street, a house which is still standing, an attractive one in good repair. Later he built an elaborate stone and brick home at the corner of his farm, at what was then Boulevard and Diamond Avenue. The grounds were meticulously landscaped with trees, shrub-

79

Woodbury Branch Library

bery, lawn stags, and statuary, some pieces of which are now in Elitch Gardens. Mr. Kennedy was active in milling, mining, and banking and was president of the school board.

The Kennedys had four sons and two daughters and, as a strong advocate of higher education, he sent all to prestige colleges. One son became a mining engineer, one a doctor, a third an attorney. The attorney, Martin H. Kennedy, was appointed by President Herbert Hoover to serve as the United States Trade Commissioner in London.

The fourth son, Horace Greeley Kennedy, rebelled

80

Woodbury mantle of handcarved basketweave oak and ornate reception hall

Denver Public Library, Western History Department Photo by Orin Sealy

Denver Public Library, Western History Department

Silas S. Kennedy's
farmhouse at 2727 Grove

93

The Kennedy mansion dominated the Boulevard

Souvenir Album, Compiled by W. A. Barbot

against academics in favor of mechanics and was a college dropout. Horace was fascinated by motorcycles and bicycles, raced in international events, and for a time traveled the RKO vaudeville circuit as a trick bike rider.

One daughter married Carle Whitehead, an attorney who had his own ideas about things others took for granted; for example, he refused to send his children to public school because they would be vaccinated. He became one of the leading Socialists in the state, fortunately after his father-in-law, Silas, of Old Guard conservatism, had died.

Silas Kennedy set up all his children in substantial homes, four of them on Federal, so that the street for a couple of blocks was a Kennedy complex. For Horace Greeley Kennedy, the motorcyclist, he built a small cottage directly across the street from his own mansion, as though Horace were put where Father could keep an eye on him. Of the five Kennedy homes, only two are still standing, that of Mrs. Whitehead with the Socialist husband and the little cottage of Horace's, the rebellious son, who, incidentally, was the grandfather of Bill Barker, contemporary author, historian, radio and television personality.

A gray stone house of Castle Rock granite, at West 34th Avenue and Alcott Street, was built by Hugh Mackay in 1891. Mr. Mackay came to Denver from the north of Scotland, where his family was in the sheep industry. He went back to Scotland six times to try to persuade his sweetheart to come to America with him. It was only after he sold property he owned "way out in

Horace Kennedy's cottage was where his father could keep an eye on him

The Hugh Mackay home, a fine example of design and stonework

Indian land," where the eastern part of City Park now is, that she would consent to leave the Highlands of Scotland for the Highlands of Denver, and he built this house for her. Mr. Mackay was active in mining and investments, and in the engineering of many of the large dams of the Rocky Mountains. The house is still in the possession of his family, little changed from its original plans, and has been named a landmark by the Denver Landmark Preeservation Commission. It has fine hand turned woodwork, stained glass windows, and is an excellent example of English-type architecture.

A home of fine Victorian features is a few blocks away

The Sayer-Brodie
house is a builder's dream

A gracious Victorian entrance

South Dakota, he opened the sandstone quarries in Lyons and was superintendent of them until 1916, when he purchased them. He found the Lyons sandstone much superior to many of the other quarries in the state and this became the largest rock quarry in western America. He also was the president of the Colorado Company, one of the state's first asphalt companies. There were ten children in the Brodie family and the three story house was ideally suited for them, with the usual parlor, back parlor, dining room, sun parlor, library, and many bedrooms, including three on the third floor instead of the usual ballroom or playroom which occupied the third floor in some of the other large houses. The home is still in the Brodie family's possession, and remains much as it was originally, except that some insensitive roofer insisted that the top of the corner tower was unsafe and should be removed, and then found it so solid that he could hardly get it off — but did, spoiling a beautiful Victorian feature.

Frederick W. Neef, who came to Denver when he was twenty-one years old, in 1873, joined his brother in the wholesale liquor and cigar business at 15th and Larimer Streets. Mr. Neef had been born in the Black Forest of Germany and was well educated, speaking and reading five languages fluently. He and his brother bought the Western Brewery at 733 Eighth Street, Denver, and renamed it Neef Brothers Brewery. Frederick built a home in Highlands at (now) 2143 Grove Street, which the family occupied until 1917. That year the company was dissolved and the brewery building later burned. One of the all too common tragedies of the time involved the Neef family. There were many small irrigation lakes and drainage ponds about the city. One such drainage pond at 22nd and Clay was a favorite skating spot, but a young Neef son fell through the ice and was drowned. The pond was drained and is now part of Jefferson Park.

The Neef house, built in 1886, has a distinctly Victorian appearance, with stained glass windows, a large carriage house, elaborate wood trim, and two intriguing but unidentified small bronze silhouettes above the front porch. The home boasts an unusual iron fence in a swirl design. The residence has been named a landmark, and stands at the end of probably the most charming two blocks (from West 22nd to West 20th on Grove) of

at 3631 Eliot Street, built in the 1880's, and owned by Colonel Daniel Sayer during the 90's. Colonel Sayer had fought with the Union forces in the Civil War, with distinguished service at the Battle of Shiloh. He was a mining man at Central City, police magistrate and attorney in Denver.

In 1908 it was bought by another of the many industrious Scotchmen who came to Highlands. John Brodie, as a young man, arrived in the United States and went first to South Dakota. His kilts, tartan of black and blue, sporran and tam were in his trunk, but his only trips back to Scotland were for business. His family in the home country owned large quarries, and when he decided to come to Colorado with the bride he married in

Rich ornamentation marks the Frederick Neef residence

Pomeroy's home with conservatory, dovecote and henhouse

Victorian and turn-of-the-century houses, unusual trees, and well-kept grounds of any in Northwest Denver.

Without a doubt, Marcus (Brick) Pomeroy was the most contradictory individual ever to hit Highlands. He seemed to delight in being contrary, which was evidenced during the Civil War when, as a newspaper editor in the state of New York, he was a "copperhead," a Confederate sympathizer. He had numerous readers but he so aroused the anger of many that a Union soldier, home on leave, entered Pomeroy's office with

the intention of shooting him. In ten minutes he left, a friend for life, a victim of Pomeroy's charismatic, almost hypnotic, personality, which showed not only in face-to-face encounters but even in his writings.

Pomeroy was nicknamed Brick, supposedly because of red hair, although he was bald in pictures taken in Denver. However, he played upon the name by building his home in Highlands at the northeast corner of Boulevard and Backus (now Federal and West 37th) all of brick imported from Omaha, and trimmed with silver-bearing rock. This was about 1880, at a time when most large expensive homes were of stone. He had a lavish brick stable to house his $3,000 team and half a dozen carriages. He was a poultry fancier and built a brick henhouse, in which each hen had a two room suite (a boudoir and setting room?).

The Pomeroy home was an elaborate three story mansion, declared to be the finest house in the Denver area. It was described as a French villa with wide tiled halls through the first and second floors. The third floor had an art and mineral gallery and a lecture room which would seat 300. Some stories say that Pomeroy never finished the house and lived in an apartment over the carriage house. If this is so, that stable apartment, we may be sure, was elaborate as was his newspaper office, furnished with plants, draperies, carpets, cushions — certainly the antithesis of most editors' offices. Other stories say that Mr. and Mrs. Pomeroy lived in gracious style in the opulent home, but only for a few months.

The house was dubbed Pomeroy's Folly. The reason isn't clear, but it obviously was not his only folly. At first glance it is hard to see what was wrong with the man, for he seemed the ideal prosperous businessman of the late 1880's, a faultless horseman, a hard worker, a dead shot with a gun, excellent with a rapier, happy and optimistic. The trouble was that, except for his newspapers, this man never earned an honest dollar in his life, according to John Kellar, close associate and biographer. Kellar said that during the years of Pomeroy's career in Denver he took from ten thousand stockholders in his various companies nearly four million dollars and not one cent was paid back to these people in dividends.

Pomeroy believed in spiritualism; in fact, he lectured on it, and said that spirits controlled his every move. These spirits must have been nefarious ones who didn't tell him the money he received should be held in company funds and not spent on his own high living and on the development of spiritualism. He promoted more than twenty-five companies interested in Colorado mining, and people poured money into them, much coming from those who were literally giving their last dollar. Some of these companies were legitimate until he bankrupted them. He grubstaked others who never bothered to cut him in on the profits. He bled the suckers and was

himself a sucker for any hard luck tale. A woman came into his office with a sob story at a time when Pomeroy himself was without a cent. He pulled the diamond stickpin from his cravat and told her to get what she could from it.

In Denver in 1880 he was publisher and editor of a weekly newspaper called *The Great West*. In it he championed the underdog and crusaded against government corruption. He paid his workers the highest wages in town. Pomeroy was against drinking or smoking, but he was a lion with the ladies. He was married three times, the first two unions ending in divorce. He apparently had numerous affairs, the details of which the press of the time discreetly refrained from giving.

Pomeroy had a brief fling at politics in Highlands, but was squelched quickly by the upright citizens of the small town. Before the elections of 1883, an open meeting was held at which, according to the bold journalism of the day, a ballot comprised of Pomeroy's "henchmen" was introduced and almost passed, before a supporter of the incumbent mayor stood up and roared out nominations for the present officials, someone else quickly moved the nominations be closed, and Pomeroy's men were left wondering what had happened.

One project of Pomeroy's was an inspiration which might have made him one of the legendary empire builders of the state. Long before David Moffat's idea for a tunnel through the Rockies, Pomeroy promoted the Atlantic and Pacific Tunnel which was to go under Mount Kelso and Grey's Peak. He felt there was enough precious metal bearing ore in the mountain to pay for the tunnel. To read his weekly, *The Great West*, one would think — and many did think — that the tunnel was through solid silver and gold, and, swept away by his seeming honesty, enthusiasm and charisma, they poured the money into his bottomless pocket. The tunnel was to be 25,200 feet long and was to be used as a railroad bore, cutting off over 200 miles in the route between Denver and Salt Lake City. A company was organized in 1881 with a capital of $7,000,000, the largest issue of stock ever made for one enterprise. Drilling began and there were only about three miles left to go when the company, plundered by Pomeroy's spirit advisers, ran out of money. Pomeroy went to New York to try to find more financing. He had raised money in every state of the union, except Colorado, where he wisely refused to sell stock.

Now the spirits deserted him and he could not find anyone to give him more money. The Panic of 1893 killed his chances of bilking more people, even his hypnotic personality failed, and he died in New York in 1896, two months before his only child, a girl, was born.

The unfinished tunnel still exists. Drilled through solid rock, it has suffered only a few small rock slides over the years. There were years of litigation brought by the stockholders. Meantime Moffat's tunnel scheme was started and the Atlantic and Pacific Tunnel was almost forgotten. More recently some engineers tried to interest Highway Department people in putting Highway I-70 through this location instead of the unstable mountain that Eisenhower Tunnel cuts, but to no avail. Owned by one man, the possible riches of the tunnel go unexplored, the entrance hidden by weeds and undergrowth. Perhaps the spirits of those bilked stockholders or those wraithlike financial advisors of Pomeroy's are guarding the tunnel from any intrusion.

Pomeroy's fabulous mansion also came to an ignominious end. In 1902 it was purchased by William Lennox of Colorado Springs for $12,500 and, given to Dean Peck of the City Temple of Institutional Society, it was named the Belle Lennox Home and used as a home for young children. In 1935 the mansion, brick stable, and brick hennery were all torn down and a drive-in eatery (now a tavern) and filling station, symbols of the mid-twentieth century, replaced the resplendent symbol of a free-wheeling happy-go-lucky swindler.

The man who built the large red brick house at the corner of 37th and Bryant Street, only four blocks from Pomeroy's, was of an altogether different ilk. John Mouat owned a lumber company in both Aspen and Denver in 1885, and was vice-president of the North Side Building and Loan Company. Both businesses failed in the Panic of 1893, and Mouat, a gentle quiet Scotchman, lived simply in South Denver after he lost his fortune. His Highlands house, though divided into apartments years ago, is little changed on the outside, built of red brick with elaborate sandstone trim, green painted stick-type porches, and its most striking feature a round turret topped with a stone rail, with large plate glass windows on the three floors. Mr. Mouat was quoted in a Denver paper in 1889, at a time when labor was striking for an eight hour day, saying, "If they want that two hours extra rest to worship God or to educate themselves, I certainly will be glad to see them get it, but if they want that much more time for loitering around saloons and drinking whiskey, I hope they will not get it." It is well that he did not know that his house was the scene of a probably drug-induced murder of two young girls in 1972.

One of the respected attorneys who lived in Highlands was William W. Anderson. Mr. Anderson, a rather small man, always wore a tall silk hat and cutaway coat, style or not. He lived with his family in a tall house on a tall hill at 2329 Eliot Street. On the morning of January 13, 1900 "Judge" Anderson put on his tall hat, walked down the eighteen steps from his house to the street, and boarded the streetcar to take him to his office at 16th and Curtis Streets, directly across the street from the *Denver Post* editorial offices. He was working at the time on an interesting case for the editors of the *Post*, Frederick G. Bonfils and Harry H. Tammen.

The *Post* had a first class "sob sister" on its staff whose pen name was Polly Pry. On an investigative trip to the penitentiary, Polly had glimpsed a sullen noncommunicative prisoner who had been there since 1883. His name was Alferd Packer, the notorious cannibal of Pitkin County, who had been found guilty of killing and eating five companions while snowbound in the winter of 1873. Packer hadn't been caught for ten years, but he had been in the penitentiary since then. Bonfils and Tammen, who loved to sponsor sensational crusades, decided Packer should be freed and hired Anderson for $1,000 to handle the legal end of obtaining a pardon.

Tammen and Bonfils were two of the most unbelievable characters in Colorado's history. Frederick Bonfils had been a small-time gambler, scalawag, and con man; Tammen was a bartender and petty confidence man. They joined talents, bought a small newspaper, and became multimillionaires. They always considered themselves above the law, were constantly involved in libel suits, and their paper was a grand example of yellow journalism. Everyone hated them, but no one would miss reading their sensational paper.

On this January morning Judge Anderson had barely

Hallie Bond

The John Mouat house represents a fortune made and lost

William W. Anderson's
tall house on a tall hill

entered his office when Polly Pry arrived. She told him that she, Bonfils, and Tammen believed Anderson had purloined money Packer had earned from his small crafts work in prison. The lawyer had never been known for a calm disposition, but he managed to bow Mrs. Pry out of his office. Then he carefully set the tall silk hat on his head and marched across the street to the *Post* offices.

Tammen and Bonfils were sitting in their private office when Anderson walked in without knocking. Polly Pry was there, too. There was some shouted name-calling. Bonfils knocked Anderson down, cutting his cheek, and ordered him from the room. Anderson brushed himself off, went out the door, then whirled and began shooting. Bonfils was struck in the throat. Tammen, cowering behind a table, was shot in the wrist and shoulder.

Anderson walked to the City Hall, went to the police desk, and said, "Arrest me. I just shot two skunks."

Anderson was an instant hero. Both his victims eventually recovered from their wounds, although Bonfils' throat was not as good as it had been. The criticism of Anderson was principally that his aim had been poor. The competitor paper, *The Denver Times,* owned and published by former Senator and Governor Thomas Patterson, blasted at the two *Post* editors with all it had. When the case was brought to trial, the jury could not reach an agreement, and a new trial had to be ordered, at which Anderson was convicted. However, men working for the *Times* found evidence that the *Post* had bribed or attempted to bribe everyone connected with the prosecution, including the jury. The *Times* accused them of perjury; *The Post* had said that Polly Pry, the only witness to the shootings, was out of town on a day when *Times* people had seen her on 17th Street. A grand jury investigated the methods used to secure Anderson's conviction. The *Times'* editorial of November 1, 1901, said, in part: "Tammen and Bonfils, Thomas [a police magistrate and crony of Tammen's] and Sadler [who had attempted to deliver the bribe money] and the others may resort to all of the legal chicanery and political skullduggery of which they, past masters in all that is vicious, and their skillful attorneys, are capable."

The grand jury did find them guilty of bribery, and a third trial was ordered for Anderson. At that one, the jury, obviously influenced by the publicity as well as the deviousness in the previous two cases, acquitted him, and Anderson continued to live his respectable life in his tall house on the tall hill until his death.

More typical of the Highlands people was the James Parks family. Mr. Parks was born in Ireland but, orphaned when young, was brought to Pennsylvania by an uncle. He fought in the Civil War and then came west, became an early buffalo hunter and was a friend of Buffalo Bill Cody. About 1868 he began work with the Union Pacific as a bridge carpenter and was a member of the original construction crew that pushed the rails from the west to meet those from the east at Ellis, Kansas. Later he was construction engineer on the building of the famous Georgetown Loop in Colorado, a railroad engineering feat.

Mrs. Parks, as was typical of many Highlands women, was active in church and club work, was a past president of the North Side Woman's Club, and served on the School Board of Arapahoe County District #17. The Parks family was distinct from other Highlands people in that their son became a governor. George, one of their two children, was appointed territorial governor of the then Territory of Alaska by President Coolidge in 1925 and re-appointed by President Herbert Hoover, serving until 1933. He had graduated from the Colorado School of Mines and worked as an engineer in Alaska where he still lives.

The Parks family originally made their home in a small frame house at 3081 West 26th Avenue, at the center of the town of Highlands. They later moved to a more up to date "Denver square" at 3347 Federal Boulevard, which had the distinction of being next door to the one which belonged to Joe Carlino, would-be bootlegging king, which was mysteriously bombed.

There is a charming one-story house, built in 1889, at 2637 West 26th Avenue, which had slipped into the anonymous background until recently when it was refurbished and turned into an attractive restaurant. The red brick structural walls, roofline, gingerbread trim on the porch, and most of the original interior woodwork have been retained. This was the home of William J. Dunwoody, president of the Dunwoody Soap Company, on 19th Street near Water Street, which was considered one of the foremost manufacturers of its kind in the United States, and one of the most important manufac-

The Dunwoody home has been rejuvenated into a restaurant

turing concerns in Denver. Mr. Dunwoody was born in Poughkeepsie, New York, where his father was also a soap manufacturer. As did so many others, William Dunwoody came to Colorado for his health, about 1883. He and his brother, Foster, organized the soap company here. His obituary in the *Denver Times* April 27, 1901, said that his business "led to an accumulation of many millions." Since obituaries of that day seemed inclined to embellish a man's story with the brightest of colors, whether he was a multimillionaire is open to question. The home, while comfortable and well built, is not the near-mansion that others built about the same time in

The Herman H. Heiser home
is an imposing landmark

The Moses home has one of the tallest red oaks in the city

Highlands. Nevertheless, he was an astute businessman who was one of those who helped develop Colorado and Denver. After William Dunwoody died when he was forty-three years old, the patent on their biggest-selling product, "Water White" soap, apparently was sold to Proctor & Gamble.

After "West Highlands," the area west of Lowell (Homer) Boulevard, was annexed in 1890, extending Highlands' west boundary to Sheridan Boulevard, construction of homes was rapid in that section.

At the corner of West 30th Avenue and Osceola Street (which was then 15th Street in Highlands) is the

Hiram G. Wolff's home is luxurious and well balanced

imposing Herman H. Heiser house. When these large homes were built, each had expansive lawns and gardens surrounding them, and the Heiser house still has magnificently tall evergreens. Herman Heiser came to Highlands from Germany by way of Wisconsin, Black Hawk and Central City. He built this house in 1893, a date that is carved over the front entrance. His monogram of HHH is in the front porch tile (and present residents say his ghost rocks in an upstairs bedroom). Mr. Heiser was in the saddlery and harness business, and his company was famous for the custom-made saddles ordered by people all over the west, made to exact dimensions to fit the

David Cox, a stone mason, built two family homes which became showcases for his skills

customer's width as well as his desires about stirrups, saddle horn, etc. His sons carried on the business. The house has a large turret on the southwest corner, large enough to be used as a bedroom on the third floor. Typical of the finer homes of the area, the woodwork, wood panelling, and doors are beautifully matched, with different woods in each room to match the furniture, such as a cherry wood room, a walnut room, a birds-eye maple room. There is a third floor ballroom. The house is designated a landmark.

A block farther west, at Perry Street and West 30th Avenue, is the William E. Moses house, built about

1895. Moses was a successful attorney and land scrip broker. He was a Civil War veteran and very active in GAR activities. He was the grand marshal of Denver's Memorial Day parade five months before his death in 1929. Mrs. Moses was a gardener and a charter member of a Denver garden club. Evidence of her hobby is a tall stately red oak, one of the tallest and oldest in the city, which reached to a height of eighty feet when measured in 1967. She also had an extensive fernery, thirty or forty feet wide, which made a dense tropical garden of the yard by the carriage house. The house itself is of red brick, with its most distinctive feature a charming little balcony off the third floor ballroom. It is not hard to imagine the romance of standing on that balcony with someone special, music playing in the background, a full moon overhead, and the lights of the city, beyond the foot of the hill, showing like the play of fluorescence in a great dark opal.

A "Denver square" is at the corner of West 30th Avenue and Newton Street, built as the home of Hiram G. Wolff, a man who was extremely influential in the building of Highlands. He was the man who had first brought water into Highlands by way of a ditch he dug himself from Clear Creek near Golden around Table Mountain. The Wolffs had a small farm and the Sunnyside Nursery on property between (now) Lowell and Newton, West 29th to West 30th Avenues, to which he brought ditch water. This property is now occupied by the Mullen Home for the Aged, Little Sisters of the Poor. As Wolff's wealth increased, principally from very successful real estate developments, he built a substantial twelve room home across the street at 3000 Newton Street. He forsook the popular Victorian style for rather plain square lines with inset front porch, and with little exterior ornamentation on the red brick structure. Built in 1891, the interior has carved woodwork, four beautiful tiled fireplaces, a library with glass enclosed bookcases, and the walls of the halls and stairways are still papered with the original heavy embossed covering. After the Wolff family moved, the house was used as a residence for Father Adam Ritter, who served as chaplain at the Mullen Home for forty years. When he left, the deed specified that the Wolff residence must be sold to a large family, and the present owners have ten children.

The "House of the Gargoyles" was built at 3425 Lowell Boulevard around 1888 by David Cox, a stone mason, for his family home. Intriguing stone carvings decorate the eaves, tops of chimneys, and spaces between windows. Dragon or gargoyle heads form downspouts. Mr. Cox built a great many of the stone buildings of the era. About 1898 he built one next door, at 3417 Lowell, and the family then lived in the new house and rented the gargoyle one. 3417 Lowell is of the more unimaginative square type, but is unusual in that the outside walls are of eighteen inch thick slabs of pink (now turned gray) sandstone from Creede, laid upright, a rare

The "new" Cox house
was uniquely constructed

The Walker home represents one of Denver's most fascinating characters

method of construction, in which cranes had to be used to lift the heavy stone. Both Cox houses are designated landmarks.

John Brisben Walker was one of the most fantastic men in the west, and he was either the owner of the large stone house at 3520 Newton Street or the lender of the money which built it. Walker attended West Point, but left to join a diplomatic mission to China, and was made a general in the Chinese army when he was about twenty years old. When he returned to this country, he invested in real estate and is reputed to have made two million dollars by the time he was twenty-six. He came to the Denver area and was superintendent of Dr. William A. Bell's Scottish-named subdivision of Highland Park. He and Bell, over the years, were closely related in a number of financial matters. In 1870, shortly after Walker arrived in Denver, he purchased a quarter section farm which he named Berkeley (see Section III). Here he developed a successful experimental alfalfa farm. He bought the farm for $1,000 and sold it for $325,000 about 1890. Walker was a handsome man, restless and moody. With the money he made from the sale of the Berkeley Farm, he went to New York City and purchased the *Cosmopolitan Magazine*, which he edited and published. Walker had had previous journalistic experiences and wrote articles and pamphlets all his adult life. Some of these revealed the bad conditions at the Chicago stockyards. Another attacked the Catholic Church, of which he had been a good member. He had given the Jesuit College, which became Regis College, fifty acres of his Berkeley Farm for a campus, and a large portrait of him had hung in the main building at Regis. However, after this attack on the church, he and his family removed themselves from the church (or were removed) and his portrait disappeared from the college.

The story is told that while he was editing the *Cosmopolitan* a lovely young lady brought a manuscript to him for publication, he fell in love with her, divorced his wife by whom he had had at least eight children, and married the second lady. The number of children Walker had by his two wives is not certain. It is known that he had nine living sons, with two others who died before reaching manhood, and one or two daughters. In his later years, during the 30's, he was married the third time.

He was considered one of the leading businessmen of New York City. Besides the magazine, he invested heavily in a number of businesses, and, with Dr. William Bell, in the Locomobile, a steam driven automobile. This was one of the fortunes that he lost, when the steam auto was replaced by the gasoline powered motor. In 1905 he returned to Denver and owned a large part of the town of Morrison and also the Park of the Red Rocks. It was he who brought Mary Garden, famed opera singer, to test the remarkable acoustics of the Red Rocks Park. He was a close friend of Mayor Robert W.

Speer and encouraged him to establish a Denver mountain parks system. Always a showman with a flair for knowing what people enjoyed, he built a popular cog railroad up Mount Morrison and arranged for Sunday afternoon trains to travel to Morrison to carry crowds of joyful excursionists to patronize the cog railroad and the town and exotic Red Rocks park.

It was in Morrison that John Brisben Walker had what might have been one of the high points of his varied career. He started to build a summer White House for presidents on Mount Falcon, out of Morrison. It was to be quite a castle with many chimneys, rooms, and fireplaces. It was not finished in 1918 when, while he and the federal government were arguing about who should pay for it, lightning struck it and it burned to the ground, leaving a ghostly ruin of stone foundations and chimneys. Walker later ran into financial troubles — not unusual in his varied career — and returned east, where he died in 1935 at the age of 88.

Bolivar Walker was an interesting person but was eclipsed by his more flamboyant brother. While John Brisben went into real estate, Bolivar went into mining, and like so many others who came west expecting to strike a bonanza, he never quite made it. He also went into the business of horse breeding and raising, but never lost his gold fever. When he was 96 years old and on his death bed, he had friends carry him on a stretcher to a mine site he owned, which he was sure would bring in riches. In the Denver city directories for many years, it is Bolivar who is listed as a resident at the house which became numbered at 3520 Newton and is a designated landmark. Originally the house was reached by a two block long sweeping driveway from West 35th and Lowell (35th was then Cumberland Avenue and Lowell was Lake Avenue and also Homer). The property had beautiful gardens, a private reservoir, and a large stable for Mr. Walker's polo ponies.

Almost every block in Highlands had an interesting family or intriguing house. There's the house that tops the tallest hill of all the hills in Northwest Denver, a three story austere place, its lines now softened somewhat by plantings. At one time considered the highest house in Denver, it stands like a sentinel at 32nd and Tennyson, watching over the slope where, until traffic became too heavy, children sledded eight blocks down

The highest house in Denver
before recent annexations

Designed by William Lang, the Ellis-Schenck home was a beauty spot for 40 years

the steep hill to Sloan's Lake in the winters, and boys tried daredevil bicycle stunts in summer. The house was the home of Dr. Samuel Robert McKelvey, a surgeon with the U.S. Public Health Service.

Seldom does one find a block like the double one between West 30th and West 32nd on Lowell Boulevard, which seemed studded with people of note. At the corner of West 32nd and Lowell there is an early shopping center, which included a drug store, dry goods company, movie theater, bakery, shoe repair shop, jeweler, grocery, and a church nearby. At the other end of the block on the west side of Lowell at West 30th, is a

Benjamin F. Stapleton's home through his first term as Denver's mayor

three story brick and shingle house designed by William Lang in 1890 for Carleton Ellis, a real estate broker in Denver who helped develop the town of Berkeley, and whose story is told in more detail in that section. Ellis lived in the Lowell house for five years or less. The address was originally Summit (West 30th Avenue) and Berkley Avenue (one of Lowell's many early names) in Wolff Place. The Ellis house was bought by Charles Meigs Schenck for his family home, and he lived there until his death in 1933 at the age of 83. Mr. Schenck was president of the Western Supply Company, secretary and general auditor of the Colorado Fuel & Iron

Company, president of the Colorado and Wyoming Railway Company, vice president of the Crystal River Railroad Company, president and treasurer of the Colorado Supply Company, which at one time operated thirty general merchandise stores in Colorado and Wyoming, and vice president and treasurer of the Merchants Fire Insurance Company. As if all these duties were not enough, he had time to serve as a member of the Denver School Board, District #1, and was treasurer of the board for twelve years, president for four or more. He was listed in *Who's Who in America*. Everyone in Highlands remembers the Schencks as having a beautiful daughter, a lovely home and garden.

The block attracted another "Who's Who," Dr. Paull Hunter, who was listed before he was forty years old. He was a physician and secretary of the State Board of Health under Governor Shafroth. However, before he became a doctor, he was a newspaper writer and foreign correspondent during the Boxer Rebellion, and always kept his newspaper connections. He was one of the founders of the Denver Press Club.

Other writers were also attracted to this block. Hattie Horner Louthan, who was an author and poet, teacher, professor of English and short story writing at the University of Denver School of Commerce, and Dean of Women there, lived in the block with her husband, Overton. Walter Juan Davis, a writer on the *Denver Post*, lived across the street. A friend of Samuel Clemens (Mark Twain), Davis entertained Clemens at his home, as did the neighbors, the Hunters.

Mayor Benjamin F. Stapleton lived at 3045 Lowell while he was Denver Postmaster and until 1930, the end of his first term of office as mayor of Denver. At 3010 Lowell Boulevard lived Edward L. Brown, educator and recognized mathematics expert. Mr. Brown was principal of North High School from 1900 to 1924, and then assistant superintendent of the Denver Public Schools until 1931. An elementary school at West 26th and Lowell Boulevard, built in 1952, is named for him.

If one drives down Lowell Boulevard, at first glance this block between 30th and 32nd seems unimpressive, the houses close together, typical turn-of-the-century two story residences. But a closer look brings to attention the big maples planted seventy-five years ago, the wide friendly porches, the flowers, the houses where the same families have lived for three generations, houses holding multitudes of memories.

William McLeod Raine was another writer who found Highlands to his liking. His first wife, Pearl Langley Raine, was a teacher at Edison Elementary School nearby, and he gave a library to the school in her name. They had a small home at 4433 West 29th Avenue. It looks like an idyllic writer's home, an out-of-the-ordinary design of stucco and half timber with gambrel roof. It is tucked in now between stores and doctors' offices.

Raine wrote over 80 western novels, with a sale of 19,000,000 copies, and more than 200 short stories and articles. Born in London, he was brought to America by his father after the early death of the wife and mother. With his three brothers, Raine tended cattle and fruit orchards — a strange combination — on his father's ranch in Arkansas, and later worked at a number of trades, including newspaper work, before he found he had tuberculosis and came to Colorado. He started to write full time in 1899. He was married three times. As his fortunes increased, he moved to a home in east Denver where he died in 1954. Raine was an early member of the Colorado Authors' League. He was a close friend of Robert Ames Bennet, whose story is told in the chapter on Berkeley. Raine's wax image greets one at the entrance of the wax museum in Denver, and he is also represented in the National Cowboy Hall of Fame.

There is another house and garden which occupied a whole block between Perry and Quitman, West Hayward Place and West 30th Avenue. It is a three story square house, with broad verandahs, now stuccoed and painted green. It was the home of William J. Carter. Carter was a wealthy lumberman from Florida, who platted and built the area from Perry to Tennyson and from West 29th to West 30th Avenue in the 1910's and 20's. He had two early auto agencies, one for the Overland and the other for the Apperson "Jack Rabbit." The house was originally red brick with a luxuriant garden. There was a home for the gardener and also one for Carter's daughter.

Of course, not all the homes of Highlands were estates. Many houses, built in the 90's, were solid middle class two story Queen Anne type, intended for solid

William McLeod Raine
lived here as he began his
writing career

William J. Carter made his first fortune in Florida, then came to Colorado for a second one

middle class citizens. Scattered among the larger ones were small ones, each with its own wooden picket or wrought iron fence, lawn, snowball and lilac bushes, a chicken house and coal shed in the back yard. Many of these houses were well built, well cared for and loved. Others were put up cheaply by developers on single twenty-five foot lots, a number of identical ones in a block. But even these small residences, usually a peaked gothic style, boasted a carved bargeboard or other wooden treatment, "gingerbread" stick porches, a front and back parlor, possibly heated by a base burner instead of a furnace, and lighted by kerosene lamps. They were almost all owner-occupied, for home ownership was a symbol of stability and security. Such were the homes of the men who made possible through their industry the building of the west. They were not "little people," that detestable supercilious term, but people who wanted the best they could afford for their families, people who were proud of their good craftsmanship, of their homes, of their wives and children. They took their politics, their churches, and their jobs seriously, and in their homes there were books, music, art, laughter, and love.

One such home, at 2914 West 29th Avenue, has been named a landmark by the City of Denver. It is a small red brick flat roofed house with a little but unique brick octagonal entrance. The original owner and builder was John Queree, who came from the Isle of Jersey, and was a skilled craftsman and inside woodwork finisher. In 1888 Mr. Queree built the house, putting the kitchen in the basement, in the style of many English homes, but his wife soon objected and a kitchen was added on the back of the house. The residence, thus altered, has remained much as it was carefully constructed by Mr. Queree, and has been cared for by the Queree's only child, Miss Pearl Queree, who was a teacher and principal in the Denver Public Schools for many years and loved by hundreds.

Scattered about Highlands are houses that were once isolated farmhouses built in the 1870's and 80's, small white frame buildings, simple but sturdy, perhaps made of woods like hemlock, which these farmers had shipped in from "back home." Indians were not far away when these houses were built, and whenever the farmwife baked biscuits, she could expect a visitation of chiefs to sit in her kitchen and eat their fill. In one instance, the chief almost insisted upon trading one of the papooses from his camp for the blonde blue-eyed baby of the family.

The area south of Sloan's Lake to West Colfax seemed remote to have been part of Highlands, but the southwest corner of the town, after 1890, was at Colfax and Sheridan, both muddy narrow dirt roads. Most of this land had been included in Thomas Sloan's land grant. (See further on page 139 .)

Small farms made up the low hill land south of the lake, along with some small homes and a few large ones. Most have been razed for business and property de-

Hallie Bond

The first year the John Querees lived in this landmark house roaming cows ate their garden

velopments, but a few remain. One interesting sturdy graystone at 1575 Yates Street was built by Gustav Winter as his family home in 1889 and was occupied by the Winters until 1918 or later. Mr. Winter was a partner in an iron fence business, and the iron cresting on his house, including a fanciful decoration at the front peak which could be a television antenna (but probably a lightning arrester), and the lacy New Orleans type iron porch trim are delightful. Another example of the beautiful iron work done by the Winter and Fitting Company is the iron gates at the entrance of Trinity Methodist Church, in downtown Denver at 18th and Broadway.

St. Anthony's Hospital, the largest institution of its

The Gustav Winter home advertised the delicate wrought iron work his firm made

kind in Colorado when it was built in 1891, was prominent on the marshy south shore of the lake, its evening angelus melodious and sheltering to the scattered but friendly neighborhood of people of many different faiths who lived nearby.

The Dickinson Library was built at Hooker Street and Conejos Place in 1913. It was an attractive building of Italian style, finished in stucco with colored medallions and frieze. The most interesting thing about Dickinson Library was the series of murals, done by Allen True, which decorated the coves of the arched ceiling. They depicted the idealized elysian life of the American Indi-

The John Springer home is nearly hidden by evergreens

ans before white man intruded on his communion with nature. Tragically, on May 7, 1953, teenagers vandalized and set fire to both Dickinson Library and Lake Junior High School. The library never reopened, but, fortunately, the murals were saved.

Long after Highlands became part of Denver, in fact, about 1915, John W. Springer had his home south of the lake at 1655 Vrain Street. The house has always had an air of mystery, a haunting, large, dark gray stucco building with tile roof, surrounded by evergreens. Mr. Springer was a popular, likeable man, well educated, and a man of many interests. He was a member of

Denver's most exclusive and prestigious clubs, a steward of Trinity Methodist Church, and a trustee of the University of Denver. As president of the Continental Trust Company, he was prominent in financial circles, and was also a lawyer, cattle and horse raiser. He was elected president of the National Livestock Association seven times. In 1904 he was the Republican candidate for mayor of Denver, defeated by Robert W. Speer. Selection by western Republicans for nomination as vice-president of the United States, to run with Theodore Roosevelt (a post which eventually went to Charles W. Fairbanks of Indiana) was another honor accorded him.

The Springers had come to Colorado in 1895 from Illinois for Mrs. Springer's health. She died in 1904. Later he married a flirtatious and beautiful lady much younger than he. Despite his efforts to make her happy with gifts and frequent trips to New York City, where she became part of the artists' scene as a model, Isabelle Springer became involved in a romance with two men at the same time. One was Tony Von Phul, a balloon racer, wine agent, and romancer of many ladies; the other was Harold Henwood, a business associate of Springer's. On May 24, 1911, Henwood stalked into the bar of the Brown Palace Hotel to find Von Phul with friends. Von Phul jumped him and Henwood started shooting wildly. Von Phul was shot three times and two bystanders were accidentally struck. The plush bar was in an uproar. Henwood walked into the onyx lobby where he was tackled and handcuffed. Von Phul and one of the bystanders later died of their wounds. The lady's name was kept out of the scandal and at the trial the romances were not revealed. Henwood was found guilty of second degree murder, but before he was sentenced, he delivered a tirade against the judge. This brought him a life sentence. He appealed to the Colorado Supreme Court, which ordered a new trial. After two years of living an easy life in a well furnished cell, he was found guilty of murder, this time in the first degree, and was sentenced to hang. Now Springer, who had divorced Isabelle, came to Henwood's rescue, saying that if he had known about his wife's lovers, he would have shot Von Phul himself. Softened by this statement, the judge changed Henwood's sentence to the original life imprisonment, and he died in prison in 1929.

Isabelle moved to New York, where she died at the age of thirty-six, reportedly of drug addiction.

Mr. Springer lived in the Sloan's Lake house, which had beautiful gardens, from approximately 1915 to 1920. In 1936 he was married again, and he and his new wife moved to an estate south of Littleton. The house by Sloan's Lake changed hands a number of times. At one time it was brightened by the name of Blossom Heath, but the evergreens have grown taller and taller to give it an ever increasing appearance of a hideaway.

Women in Highlands

Life in Highlands in the 80's and 90's was much like that in any town in those years, without the rowdy and drunken elements. It was not a leisurely life. The wealthy and well-to-do had servants to help care for the big houses with their bric-a-brac, carved woodwork, potted palms, starched linens, polished brass and silver. The less affluent in their smaller homes often had a spinster or widowed relative living with them, who might earn a bit of money as a dressmaker or milliner, but in addition she shared the housework, the baking, the cooking, the canning, the washing and ironing. Evenings were taken up, for the women, with bedtime stories to the children and then "relaxing" needlework — mending, sewing, embroidery, crocheting, knitting, tatting.

Most of the ladies' lives revolved around their homes and their churches, and certainly they played a big part in making the church an effective influence in their family lives. Church attendance, the women's societies or the prayer meetings, Sunday School, ice cream socials and church dinners, plus the men's lodge activities, made up the bulk of the social life outside the home. At home there were gatherings around the piano which evolved, in the ballrooms of the affluent, into musical or elocution recitals plus teas and "at homes."

The years of Highlands' great advance were also the years of women's advance. Movements for women's suffrage were gaining in momentum all over the country, and Highlands was no exception. Women knew that home and social life was not enough. They felt they were too intelligent, and in many cases too well educated, to be relegated to the kitchen and parlor, the sewing box and recipe book, with no other activities but church. In 1895 women of Highlands formed the North Side Woman's Club for "mutual improvement and cooperation in all that pertains to the good of humanity." They soon were deep into charity work and cultural activities, and still continue to be active in these lines.

Women individually, as well as collectively, were doing things. They had received the vote in 1894 in Colorado. Immediately the suffragette movement leaped into politics, and possibly more women filled seats in the legislature in the next few years than they have at any other time. Highlands' contribution was Harriet G. R. Wright, who served two years in the legislature, beginning in 1899. Mrs. Wright, like many other Highlands women, had been educated at a female seminary, was married and had children, in Mrs. Wright's case four sons. Her husband was involved in business in both Boulder and Denver. She was very much interested in equal suffrage for women and wrote many articles on suffrage, as well as stories and sketches. She was active in public life for thirty-five years and was prominent in club, church and philanthropic work. She served four and a half years as a member of the board of control of the State Industrial School for Girls, and was in the office of the Superintendent of Public Instruction in 1913-14. Mrs. Wright died in California in 1928. When she was active in politics in Colorado her family home was at 3347 West Moncrieff Place.

All households, rich and poor, suffered what we would consider today the most onerous of tasks. Kerosene lamps, no matter how expensive, how decorated with roses embellished with crystal pendants and touches of gold, smelled. There were smoky lamp chimneys to clean each day. Highlands did not have gas lights as did some other parts of the city but some of the wealthy had electricity, which was uncertain or fluttering, so oil lamps were always handy. Of course, appliances were nonexistent. Ironing was done with a sad iron heated on the back of a stove, even on the hottest days; and it consisted of ironing yards of delicately pleated underskirts and waists, little boys' dresses (worn until they were three or four), older boys' and men's shirts, and, of course, the women's and girls' full skirted petticoats and dresses. Many a housewife dis-

Ornate kerosene lamp

proved the maxim that ladies didn't sweat, in a day long before deodorants were invented.

The wealthy and lower class alike had problems of moths in the carpets, ants in the cupboards, mites in the cheese, clinkers in the stoves and furnaces. They had either to supervise or do the jobs of polishing stoves, carrying out ashes and putting them in ashpits for the ash hauler, who came periodically and who cleaned the pits and hauled away the ashes for a dollar or two. There were the problems of trying to prevent or remove perspiration odors and stains from non-washable clothing or the shine from a good black skirt or blue serge suit.

They all shared the fear of diseases, for medicine was rudimentary and household remedies were sometimes as satisfactory as the powders and elixirs mixed by the physician or pharmacist. But surely medical knowledge was far ahead of some of these crude home remedies found in the *Handy Cyclopaedia of Everyday Wants* dated January 1, 1893:

"For asthma: 2 oz. best honey and 1 oz. castor oil. Take 1 tsp. night and morning.

Baldness: 2 oz. spirits of wine, steep 2 drachma of cantharides [Spanish fly] pulverized. Set 2 to 3 weeks, filter, mix with cold hog's lard. Scent. Rub into head every morning and evening.

Bronchitis: occasionally suck a small piece of common salt petre and swallow juice.

Cancer (a sure cure): take common wood sorrel, bruise it on brass, spread it in the form of a poultice and apply as long as a patient can bear, then apply bread and milk poultice until patient can bear wood sorrel again. Continue this until the cancer is drawn out by the roots.

Colic: take a teaspoon of salt in a pint of water, drink and go to bed. It is one of the speediest remedies known. It will revive a person who seems almost dead from a heavy fall.

Hemorrhages of lungs can be instantly cured by throwing into the mouth from a vial one or two teaspoons of chloroform. It will give instant relief to the greatest suffering and stop the most severe case of bleeding of the lungs.

Sleeplessness: upon retiring to bed, eat 3 or 4 small onions.

Smallpox: I am willing to risk my reputation if the worst case of smallpox cannot be cured in three days, simply by use of cream of tartar. One ounce of cream of tartar in pint of water drank at intervals is a certain never-failing remedy. It has cured thousands, never leaves a mark, never causes blindness, and avoids tedious lingering."

Doctors, of course, struggled against such drivel and fought to help the tubercular, the women suffering in childbirth, the injured, the sick. The towns of Northwest Denver were the residences of many doctors, some with downtown offices, some with offices in their homes. All drove horses and buggies, later little black coupes, to make house calls, to deliver in home bedrooms babies "brought in their little black bags," and to aid wherever they could.

Rare exceptions to the standard picture of the 1890's were at least two women doctors, a profession frowned upon for females. Each attended Boston University Medical School and they shared both office and home. Dr. Mary Ford was born in Pittsburgh, and, after graduating from medical school, practiced in Pittsburgh and in Chicago for two years. She came to Colorado in 1898 and made her home in Highlands until she died in 1951. Dr. Ford was an efficient professional woman, who never married. Her brisk exterior dissolved into a gentle kindness with a hurt frightened child or any sick patient. Like so many doctors, she was so poorly paid that she often could not take care of her taxes and had to be saved from a tax sale of her home by friends.

Dr. Ford's first Highlands home was at (now) 3626 West 32nd Avenue, a house presently hidden by store fronts. About 1900 she moved to 3827 West 32nd Avenue and stayed there until her death in 1951. The house, a large two and a half story red brick, had been built by W. F. R. Mills, a successful Denver businessman who later became Denver's Manager of Improvements and Parks in 1916 under Mayor Robert Speer. When Mayor Speer died in 1918 Mr. Mills filled the balance of the term as mayor. He did not run for re-election, but was appointed head of the Water Board, where he served for four years.

There was an adequate yard for Dr. Ford to spend her few spare hours with her flowers, accompanied by her big collie, and in back is a large stable where she kept and cared for her horse, which she would harness to a buggy for house calls. Later she drove an old Dodge. The property had one of the many artesian wells of Highlands, and Mr. Mills had piped the water to a number of homes in the neighborhood.

Dr. Helene Byington was a widow. Her husband had been an educator in Colorado Springs and Boulder, serving as superintendent of schools and also as a professor at both University of Colorado and Colorado College. When he died, she took her two small daughters with her and entered Boston Medical School. Probably the two women doctors met there. She and Dr. Ford established a joint office and practice in downtown Denver, with Dr. Byington specializing in women's and children's diseases. The two women and two children shared their home until 1907 when Dr. Byington died suddenly while in Montrose.

Dr. Byington's younger daughter was named Spring, a

Dr. Mary Ford was a
mainstay of the community
but often could not afford
her taxes

bright pretty blonde youngster with a twinkle of humor and mischief in her eye which she never lost. Spring's parents had once been quite interested in amateur theatricals and one summer, possibly to keep her out of mischief for the vacation, Dr. Byington asked Mary Elitch if Spring might act in the Elitch Theatre. Spring went on to become one of the country's busiest, most beautiful, and beloved character and comedy actresses. Always feminine and chic in appearance, she became the prototype "fluttery mother" character. She made more than 75 motion pictures, acted in thirty Broadway plays, and toward the end of her life she acted in the television series "December Bride," which ran for five years and was in the top ten shows. She never would reveal her age, but those who attended North High School with her knew she must have been born around 1892, which would have made her 79 years old at her death in 1971.

Fun in Highlands

While there were blemishes under the surface of Highlands' moral virtue — an illicit love affair, a family quarrel, a neighborhood misunderstanding, "wild" youths who usually grew up to be the same moralistic persons their parents had been — taken as a whole Highlands was a very respectable town. They were in some ways snobbish. People in Highlands east of Lowell looked down on those west of Lowell. All in Highlands considered themselves superior to the other suburbs and most definitely to Denver.

But they did have good clean fun. They raced their fine horses along tree lined Boulevard, sometimes getting a speeding ticket. They had their bicycle clubs and their formal dancing clubs. And they had the amusement parks.

Amusement parks

In the 1880's and 90's amusement parks began to spring up like dandelions, largely because of the advent of electricity. River Front Park, Denver's earliest amusement park, was unbelievable, except that anything was believable in that growing metropolis built on dreams, preposterous hopes, burgeoning fortunes, wide open sin, and moralistic religions. The park had as varied and colorful a story as did its founder, John Brisben Walker. Although the park was in Denver, it deserves to be mentioned in this story because of Walker's connections with the northwest suburbs.

He founded the River Front Park along the southeast side of the Platte River on nine city blocks running from 15th to 19th Streets. This area was already well known to early Denverites where, even before the arrival of the white man, the Arapahoes had pitched their tents in winter camp and held their ritual dances. A grove of cottonwoods here at the river's edge became a picnic spot for the early newcomers, and on July 4, 1876 it was the place of celebration when Colorado became a state.

When Walker bought the area, he envisioned something newly different. Ornate saloons, gambling halls, and parlor houses existed in Denver for the racier crowds, but Walker visualized a pleasure resort for the families of the spreading town, to be made beautiful with flowers, grass, and trees, a place of clean sports, entertainment, and fun. This was ten years before Coney Island, New York's famous amusement park, was founded.

The land Walker owned seemed an unlikely spot for such a resort. It had been considered part of the bed of the river which periodically flooded. Walker ditched the stream to confine it to its channel, woods were cleared off, grass and some alfalfa, in which Walker was interested, were planted in geometric beds. A grandstand which would seat 5000, facing a half mile oval race track and baseball diamond, was built. There were quarters for 100 horses. A straight boating course in the river was promised; tennis courts and a gymnasium at the foot of 15th Street were built. The grounds were brightly lighted by electricity, a marvel of itself at that time.

On July 4, 1887, 2000 people gathered at River Front for an ox barbecue which marked the park's opening. It was a hot day, and all improvements had not been finished so the paths and roads were dusty, but there were drills and maneuvers by the cavalry, an independent German military company and high school cadets, and there was plenty to eat for the boisterous crowd.

By September when an exposition of Colorado's products opened at the park, a transformation had been made by plantings where there had been a wilderness of

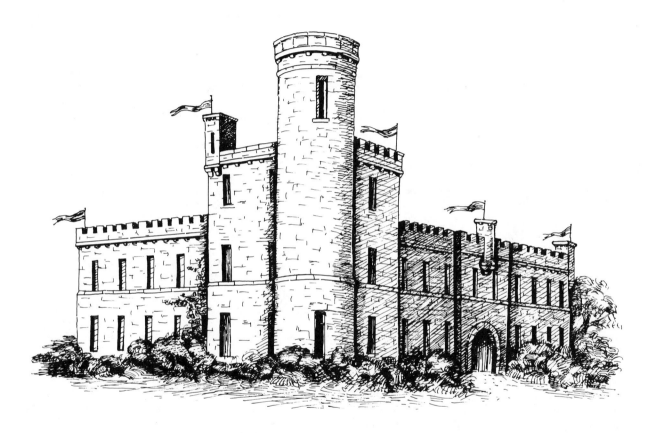

Diane Lauen

Castle of Commerce at River Front Park

weeds and bushes. Gravel walks had been laid out. Multitudes of Colorado's agricultural products were exhibited and there were opening exercises by local dignitaries and a grand parade.

What proved to be the most permanent part of the park was a sprawling three story stone castle situated at the gate. Like a Rhine castle, it had round towers and large circular doorways, which needed only a chained drawbridge to make real the illusion of medieval grandeur. It was built as an exhibition hall and also housed a permanent mineral exhibit. It was always called the castle, and years after the rest of the park faded it stood as a symbol of mystery and romance, much more than it did of mineral exhibits and county fair type competition in farm and kitchen products.

River Front was always busy. Whenever people thought of athletic events or band concerts, they thought of River Front. Wild west and rodeo performers, trap shooters, boomerang throwers, all exhibited their skills here. Horse racing had been a regular entertainment for Denverites since the earliest settlers had pitted mounts against each other. Now racing stock was refined, excitement was rampant, betting was genteel, and races were duly reported in the newspapers. Nighttime races of three horse chariots were held under electric lights as well as in the daytime.

In one Roman chariot race a team became runaways, completely out of control. Into the stretch they came, two full lengths ahead of the others. Four more times they circled the track, bettering their time on each lap. Foam flowed from the horses' mouths, sweat covered their bodies. The spectators were frenzied. The driver futilely pulled on the reins with all his strength. Several men finally managed to stop them. The driver had to be pried from the vehicle and taken to the hospital.

Six day walking races, a phenomenon of the times, were held at River Front Park, as well as at other parks about the city. There always seemed to be one favorite racer, handsome, personable, and flirtatious, for whom everyone — especially the ladies — cheered and whose clique of rooters followed him from place to place.

Bicycle racing was a popular sport in Denver in the 90's and early 1900's, as it was all over the country. While contests were held everywhere, up mountain canyons, cross country, down hazardous hills, on dusty prairie roads, the River Front track was choice. Several exclusive cycling clubs were formed among the young men of the city and each had its own club rooms or club houses. One, the Ramblers, met in the castle at River Front.

Baseball games were overwhelmingly attended by excited and loyal supporters of the local or visiting teams. The grandstands were packed for the scheduled Sunday afternoon thrillers. Teams came from Colorado Springs, Pueblo, Leadville, Georgetown, Aspen, and even from other states. The story is told of one game at River Front between the Chicago White Stockings and the All-Americans where one play was not a grandstand but a bandstand play. A portable bandstand was drawn to the side of the diamond during games. In this particular instance a high fly headed for the bandstand, and an outfielder leaped onto the stage to catch it, to the roar of the crowd.

Walker was one of the most enthusiastic supporters and gave free beer to the team that won. At another game, when a winning run was made, it so excited Walker that he rushed into the castle, where an agricultural fair was in progress, grabbed up nine pies from an exhibit, and presented one to each of the players on the winning team.

A lively winter sport was that furnished by the Denver Toboggan Club. On January 5, 1888 they opened their toboggan slides at River Front. These were about a thousand feet in length, skimming fourteen feet above the top of the grandstand. Each slide was four feet wide and the incline was covered with roofing felt. Eighteen hose nozzles sprayed the slides each night. Tobogganists climbed a stairway to the top, a starter tripped the levers, and the steel shod toboggans would travel up to 180 miles an hour. Some brave — or foolhardy — young men dared to go down the slides on home made barrel stave skis. A skating rink was also opened, and they thoughtfully provided well heated "retirement rooms for ladies" where hot chocolate and coffee were served.

The bandstand was wheeled into the center of the track for what were called the most important musical events which ever occurred in Denver (in 1888), concerts by the famous Gilmore band. The previous year another famous band, Cappa's, had opened the park. For the Gilmore concerts Walker arranged for a new streetcar line to make a circle trip up 17th Street, across on Curtis to 15th, down to the gates of the park, to prevent disappointment to the estimated twenty thousand ticket holders in reaching the park.

River Front had some of the most remarkable fireworks displays ever seen in the west, extravaganzas with hundreds of actors and convincing sets, such as the Last Days of Pompeii, the Siege of San Sebastopol, the Fall of Rome. Grandstand seats were sold as well as seats on the balcony of the castle, which went to favored guests. It was heady entertainment for a town just emerging from frontier status.

One summer Walker had the Platte dammed at 19th Street to form a small lake and on it floated a steamboat on which plays and musicals were presented. The first Sunday night the town marshal and his deputies boarded the boat, graciously allowed the customers to see the show (thus also seeing it themselves) and then arrested the manager. Baseball games on Sundays were all right, but theatrical performances — no!

By 1890 Walker's business interests had shifted to New York and he attempted to sell off River Front Park to the city, but citizens couldn't see why such a rich man as Walker couldn't just give it to the city. An ad he placed in the *Rocky Mountain News* November 22, 1891 stressed that it was only three minutes by cable car to the leading banks of the city, and that the Exposition Building, 64 feet wide by 125 feet long, was an excellent piece of stonework and of design suitable for nearly all kinds of manufacturing, storage, etc. Union Pacific Railroad bought the property, or at least part of it, in 1891 for $1,200,000. As the railroads expanded in the area, River Front became an undesirable place, dirty with soot and smoke, and, without that promotional hand of Walker's, the park, which was still trying to struggle along, steadily declined.

In 1894 the people of Highlands looked down from their homes on the hills to a pitiful sight at River Front. Here many ragged, destitute men were gathering, miners from the mountains, laborers from the towns — all men without jobs and without money, products of the Panic of 1893. They formed the Denver section of Coxey's Army, that poorly organized disastrous march on Washington in the summer of 1894. The city of Denver gave them lumber with which they built 130 rafts. On a June day, after many delays and false starts, they set out on the South Platte, swollen by spring run-offs. Thirteen were reported drowned before they reached Brighton.

In 1899 the Women's Clubs of Denver were using the park for recreational facilities for children of the slums. That spring Ringling Brothers Circus had arrived at River Front with a 65 car train of fabulous circus magic; but the women who opened their summer camp for the children in June complained bitterly that the elephants had torn up the new grass, the animals had fouled the ground, and much trash had been left on the site.

At last the River Front grandstand burned, and the castle was left alone with ghosts and memories of brighter nights, now with only the moon to illuminate its broken windows, papers and tumbleweeds to skitter around its corners with every wind. To add to its macabre aura, in 1899 a rejected suitor shot the girl he loved and left her body in the weeds near the castle, then went on to commit suicide. The glory of River Front Park was gone, the castle was reduced to being used as a washroom for railroad men and as a hay storage warehouse. It finally burned in the 1950's. But River Front was only the prologue to other fun places.

The story of Elitch Gardens has been told and will be retold many times, but no account of Northwest Denver would be complete without repeating the high points of the Gardens' history. Elitch Gardens was a spot of magic, wisps of which still linger on moonlight nights about the flower beds, under the venerable trees, around the corners of the Victorian cafe and the famous theater. Only wisps but they are there for those who hunt for them.

Elitch's was the expression of a gracious and lovely person, Mary Elitch, still known as the lady of the Gardens. Mary Hauck, convent educated, was a beautiful sixteen year old when she eloped in California with a strapping handsome actor, John Elitch. They came to Colorado and soon opened a fine restaurant at 15th and Arapahoe, later known as Tortoni's. In order to provide fresh fruits and vegetables for their tables and to provide themselves with a gracious home, they bought the Chilcott Farm at West 38th Avenue and Tennyson Street (then Prospect Avenue and Canby Street).

There was already a thriving apple orchard on the farm, and John immediately set about laying out walks, planting flower beds, and converting his farm into a park. John had theater in his blood and his dream was to do something in Denver in the theatrical line. A zoological garden, incorporated into a family resort, seemed the answer.

On May 1, 1890 the Gardens opened to throngs of people. Mayor Wolfe Londoner of Denver opened the gates with a speech, cut short by a spring rain. Phineas T. Barnum and Mr. and Mrs. Tom Thumb were guests that day, and always remained loyal friends of Mary Elitch. There were free vaudeville acts which John or-

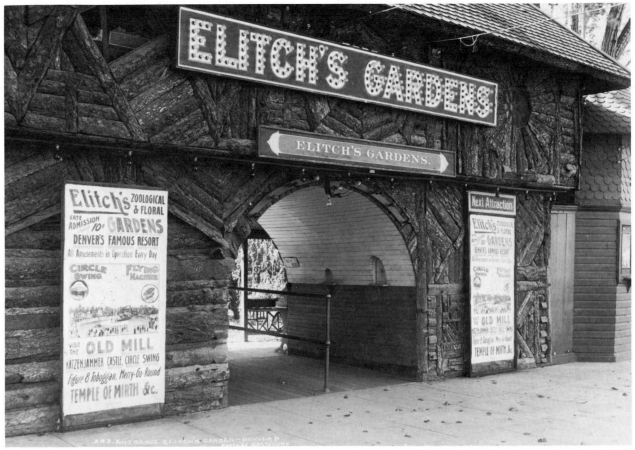

The rustic gate to Elitch Gardens

ganized and offered. From that day on the tone of Elitch's was established — wholesome, clean, and joyful entertainment.

The Elitch farm, turned amusement park, in 1890 was way out in the country. People came by horse and buggy, farm wagons, horseback, afoot. Some managed to crowd onto a steam motor line railway which ran to the Berkeley Resort at Berkeley Lake, going past Elitch's gate. The end of the Denver cable lines was at the present West 30th Avenue and Zuni Street, and some

people walked the two miles to the park. By the next summer the West End Electric had built a line up Sheridan Boulevard to Elitch's, and success was assured.

That first winter of 1890-91 John Elitch took a troupe of minstrels to tour California. While in San Francisco the big husky man who had never been sick contracted pneumonia and died. Heartsick Mary looked at the shattered dream of a family resort and concluded all she could do was to carry on as John would have wished.

During the next thirty years Mary was Elitch Gardens.

This steam train
brought customers to Elitch's

West End Electric cars
served Manhattan Beach
and Elitch's

Elitch's open porch theatre, the smallest train in the world in the foreground

Gracious and dearly loved by everyone, she developed the theater into a stock company theater which was known the world over and is now the oldest continuously operating summer theater in the country. Her greatest loves were the theater, her flowers, all children and animals. Her friends were those whose names still shine in entertainment history — P. T. Barnum, Sarah Bernhardt, Mrs. Fiske, David Warfield, Douglas Fairbanks, and hundreds more. The greatest and mightiest in the world of drama acted in her theater. Her flowers were unexcelled and the formal gardens of today are just as Mary laid them out. Parents brought their children on the free Children's Day each week and left them for the day with their fairy godmother, Mary Elitch, secure in the knowledge they would be well cared for.

Mary, in a way, never grew up. She believed in a fairyland and laughter. Because of her trusting lovable way, people wanted to do things for her, which helped make her a leading business woman of the day. She was not to be disappointed, and children found in her a kindred spirit whom they instinctively trusted and loved. She was the princess in a dainty pink dress and large picture hat who met them at the gate on their special day. In a two wheeled cart drawn by a trained ostrich she drove about the gardens. She entertained by going into the bear pit to feed a favorite bear and put him through his tricks. She provided pony rides, a merry-go-round, the smallest train in the world on which the children could ride, playgrounds, free dancing classes.

For the adults, besides the theatre, there were picnic spots in the orchard, vaudeville performances, Indian Club champions, pantomimists, jugglers, a bicycle loop-the-loop, the famous Ivy Baldwin to do aerial acrobatics and balloon ascensions.

The Elitch zoo was the first in Denver. It had ostriches, bears, giraffes, camels, lions, kangeroos, wild cats, deer, antelope, water buffalo, monkeys, snakes — and Mary loved them all. In the winter when the Gardens were quiet and deserted, she would slip out of her bungalow in the Park to see that the animals were safely protected against the blizzards. Mary's sense of humor saw her through what might have been traumatic incidents of animals getting loose from their cages and frightening patrons, or even marauding and causing havoc in her own home or wandering onto the theater stage.

The animals and all the children of Denver were the children of her own that she never had. The theater and its actors were her love.

Mary saw a need for more cultural outlets for the people of Denver, and for many seasons she presented symphony and band concerts in the theater or under the trees. Mrs. Elitch insisted upon operating her gardens on clean, strictly moral standards. There was a penny arcade which showed animated pictures, but one can be sure there were never any teasingly off-color pictures shown. At one time when she was out of the city, the citizens nearby lamented that if Mary Elitch were at home, she would fight against a liquor license applica-

The matinee crowd
at Elitch theater

Denver Public Library, Western History Department Photo by L. C. McClure

Mary Elitch went into
the bear pits to feed them

Library, State Historical Society of Colorado

The miniature train was built absolutely true to scale

tion for a beer garden across 38th from the Gardens, for she would tolerate no rowdiness either in or near her park. Of course, Elitch's was within Highlands, the blue law town, but Mary would not have permitted liquor in the Gardens, law or not. In fact, no liquor was ever served in the Gardens until the 1940's when a cocktail lounge was opened. There was a strong flavor of respectability and gentility that permeated the Gardens, and Mary promised that no girl would ever find herself in a compromising situation at Elitch's.

In 1900 Mary Elitch married Thomas D. Long, who was manager of the Gardens. They went on a trip around the world for a honeymoon and were feted everywhere, for Mary was internationally famous as the only woman amusement park operator in the world.

Mary Elitch-Long, as she was now known, continued with her husband to manage the Gardens for several more years. In 1916 the pastoral innocence she had depicted in her amusement park was lost to the clouds of a World War. The war was hard on all amusement parks, but Elitch's struggled through. Many of the animals had died of old age. Others were given to City Park Zoo. The bears finally were all that were left. Because building materials were hard to get, the Gardens became run down.

Faced with a decrepit park and probable bankruptcy, Mary had to make the heart-breaking decision to sell her beloved Gardens. *The Denver Post* wanted to buy it for their Sells-Floto Circus, but she sold it to others who employed John M. Mulvihill to manage it. In a few years Mulvihill bought all interest.

Apparently Mary had other personal worries, for it was rumored that her marriage to Thomas Long was not a happy one. On September 14, 1920, Mr. Long was killed in an auto accident a few miles north of Colorado Springs.

Mary Elitch-Long made two stipulations to the new owners of her beloved park; first, that the name of Elitch Gardens would never be changed, and, second, that she might maintain her home in the Gardens as long as she lived. Those two promises were not broken.

She stayed in her bungalow, located at about the site of the present Calypso fun ride, a new home which had replaced her little Victorian cottage. In the summer she could look out at the people, enjoying their pleasure. The winters were lonely and quiet, too quiet, but peopled with precious memories. She did not leave until 1932 when she moved to her sister and brother-in-law's home across West 38th Avenue. There she died in 1936, and all the children who had grown up in her park and theatrical people over the world mourned their beautiful lady of the gardens.

Mr. Mulvihill and his successor, his son-in-law, Arnold B. Gurtler, and later the Gurtler sons, carried on many of the traditions of the park. It is still a picnic spot and the flower gardens are still beautiful. The zoo is gone, and Children's Day has become Kiddieland, with many fascinating rides. The Elitch bungalow for a few years was turned into a spook house before it was razed. The baseball diamond and grandstand have long been gone in favor of a parking lot.

There have been tragedies. The $200,000 Monitor and Merrimac show burned one night in the early 1920's. One hot afternoon in July, 1944, the Old Mill burned with a loss of six lives. There have been fatal accidents on some of the wild thrilling rides.

But there has been romance. In fact, it is a safe estimate to say that over the years seventy-five per cent of the romances in Denver either started or were fostered at the Gardens.

A large dance hall, the Trocadero, was built about 1922. A gray stucco building, quite cavernous, it had open arches on all sides which brought the magic of the Gardens in and sent the beguiling music across the park. The floor was free-floating on a cushion of horsehair pads to be particularly resilient. During the days of the Big Bands in the 30's and 40's the Troc was packed every night. In the Great Depression days dances were a nickel a piece, and long stag lines, both men and girls, filled the wide side corridors separated from the dance floor by an iron fence. This was a phenomenon peculiar to those moneyless days. Young men not able to afford to date and girls eager to dance gathered in separate groups and surreptitiously looked each other over. Sometimes two girls would dance together, mostly to demonstrate their terpsichorean abilities; others hoped their vivacity and pretty faces would entice certain ones they had already spotted in the male group to spend their precious nickels on a dance. They were a well behaved group, and Elitch's practiced their protection of respectability even under these circumstances. If a couple danced too intimately, perhaps cheek to cheek, there would be a discreet tap on the man's shoulder by one of the Garden's non-uniformed "chaperones" who roamed the floor. The men were required to wear suits and ties, and no active dances such as a "jitterbug" were allowed, but a wave of happy humanity drifted and swayed counter-clockwise around the floor to the tunes of Dick Jurgens, Sammy Kaye, Wayne King, the Dorseys, Les Brown, Glenn Miller, and many other big name bands. During World War II men in uniforms and their dates crowded the floors.

During the 50's and 60's styles of dancing changed and, to the regret of thousands of nostalgic romantics whose loves blossomed under the pink and mauve decorations of the Trocadero, the building was razed at the end of the 1975 season, and replaced by fountains and gardens.

The most unchanged buildings about the Gardens are the turreted and screen porched Orchard Cafe, which

The Trocadero at Elitch's

carried on the wish of John Elitch, the restaurant man; and the theatre, somewhat rebuilt for fire protection but still exhibiting the autographed portraits of all the greats who performed there, and the faded stage curtain showing "Anne Hathaway's cottage a mile away/Shakespeare sought at close of day."

The south side of the park, where Mary Elitch once leisurely rowed a boat on the waters of a small artificial lake, is dominated by carnival rides of every description, and the screams of the riders and the whistle of the modern little train filter into the theatre.

Today there's an incongruity between the theatre-bound long-skirted ladies with men in coats and ties, mixed with picnicking families in shorts and sport shirts, or groups of denims and sandal-clad young people waiting in line at the rides. The little children, inevitably grubby from picnic meals, cotton candy, and many rides, do not bear much resemblance to the boys and girls in starched dresses and white shirts, white shoes and socks, and sailor hats, whom Mary Elitch loved, but we can be sure she would have loved these just as much. And among the flower beds, the few apple trees that remain, the fountains, the statuary — yes, there are still wisps of that fairyland wonder that was Mary Elitch.

Perhaps of all Colorado amusement parks, Manhattan Beach's history is the most catastrophic. It sprang from a flood and died in a fire.

On a day in 1861 pioneer farmer Thomas M. Sloan, on the South Golden Road, had watched in amazement and concern as the water in the well he had dug the day before on the north end of his farm overflowed and flooded the long dry prairie valley where it was located. Word of the gushing well spread to the fledgling town of Denver. People rode out on horseback to see the phenomenon of Farmer Sloan's well and talked as they watched the water spread.

"Why, this has been a dry valley, dry as an ashpit. The stage road to Georgetown ran through here."

Indians stood and watched, then rode away. This valley, inexorably filling with water, had long been their favorite playground with a pony race track and war games area.

When the water stopped running, Farmer Sloan had a lake of 200 acres on his farm, and the history of that part of the country, three miles west of the settlement of Denver, was forever changed. The undeveloped rural lake was used by Denverites for swimming, boating, fishing. Thomas Sloan found that he was an inadvertent squatter instead of a landowner. The ground had previously been given by President Lincoln in bounty grant for military services to a Mrs. Deborah Boggs, widow of a private who had served in the Massachusetts militia and had lost his life in the War of 1812. Mrs. Boggs never saw her land way out in the wild west, but Thomas Sloan had to go through legal proceedings to secure it from her heirs, as well as from other men who also claimed land grant rights. Sloan developed a prosperous

farm and had an ice house on the shores of his lake, selling ice as far away as Cheyenne. But in 1872 he sold out and moved to Pueblo.

In 1874 an I. M. Johnson purchased eighty acres along the north rim of the lake, hoping to establish a formal park with trees, lawns, flower beds, fountains, pools with swans afloat, buggy trails and promenades where ladies and gentlemen, dressed in their 19th century finery, could ride, stroll or court. To introduce his plans he hosted a party of influential citizens. The party was a success, but the ambitious project went begging for lack of financial backing.

At the same time an exciting undertaking was developing a mile east of the lake at what is now 17th Avenue and Federal Boulevard. The Grandview Hotel, a large square frame structure, stood there on a high promontory above the Platte River. It was served by a horse car line which carried Denver people from 15th and Larimer Streets across railroad tracks and the Platte River, up the steep hill to a turntable at the hotel front. In 1874 the Boulevard Canal Company dug a canal from a lagoon lying just south of this hotel to Sloan's Lake. The channel was 30 feet wide and deep enough to accommodate a small steam launch.

Property owners along the way, fearing water seepage into their cellars, asked for a court injunction to stop the canal construction. The company heard of the injunction which was to be served on a Monday, and hired every man they could find to work all day Sunday. At sunset Sunday, May 3, 1874, the canal was finished. The level of the lake went down four feet as the canal filled. The next day a low area east of the lake had also filled with water, called Cooper's Lake. Years later the two lakes were joined so that Sloan's Lake assumed a figure on maps that looks rather like a Mexican maraca.

When the canal and boat were ready, special launching ceremonies were held at the Grandview Hotel. There were speeches and music as dignitaries boarded for the initial ride. The banner-bedecked boat was christened *The City of Denver*. Her captain turned on the engines and the main pump blew out, spewing water all over the dignitaries and crew. It was a few weeks before she was repaired and ready to make the run. The trip was a popular one all summer, with people making the com-

Grand View Hotel at
17th and Federal, 1874

The new *City of Denver*
carried 150 people

bined horsecar-steamboat excursion for 25¢, but the canal company was plagued by financial troubles and lawsuits because of residential floodings. In November of the same year a very small item in a Denver newspaper announced that *The City of Denver* was sold at sheriff's auction for $240. Evidently it was run for at least one more year, for in *Across the Meridians,* a privately published diary of Harriet E. Francis, the wife of a diplomat making a round-the-world trip, there is a notation: "Denver, June 28, 1875. There is a canal or artificial river, one mile long, just outside the city, called 'The Inland Sea' where a pretty miniature steamer makes frequent trips."

During the next few years the lake lay dormant, visited only by ice cutters and skaters in the winter, by picnickers in the summer. During these years rowboats were rented at the lake by various individuals. In the early 1880's Mr. Henry Lee, who was a resident of Highlands at what is 2653 West 32nd Avenue, and who was a member of the Colorado House of Representatives, introduced a bill to the Third General Assembly to purchase the acreage of Sloan's Lake and Edgewater, the village on its west shore, to create a large Denver park. The House passed the measure but the Senate voted it down, buying instead the south half of what is now Denver City Park. Sloan's Lake many years later did become, with surrounding land, a Denver city park.

In 1890 the city of Highlands annexed the area from Lowell Boulevard (then Homer) their original western boundary, as far west as Sheridan Boulevard, which was the county line between Arapahoe and Jefferson Counties. (All of the Denver area at that time was in Arapahoe County, a county which as first surveyed stretched from Jefferson County to the Kansas state line.)

In the winter of 1889 a German immigrant, Adam Graff, cutting ice at the lake, dreamed of a family resort such as he had known in Germany, to be built on the north shore of the lake. He immediately set about to make his dream a reality and the next summer, 1890, Sloan's Lake Resort opened. It had a fresh air pavilion seating 3000 people. There were 40 rowboats, a couple of sailboats, and a new *City of Denver*, which was a converted forty foot coal barge bought by Adam Graff at the Mississippi and brought across the plains on wagons. It could carry 150 people.

Adam Graff's dream had budded, but it barely had time to bloom when, in April, 1891, the grand pavilion and refreshment building burned to the ground. Graff and his associates sold the dream and the holdings to a new company formed by an eastern syndicate who renamed it Manhattan Beach.

The Manhattan Beach Company brought the area into its greatest glory. The sale was completed April 22, 1891, and the new owners wasted no time preparing for their official June opening. During May 10,000 trees and shrubs and 500 potted palms were set out. Formal flower gardens were designed and planted. Work was begun on an auditorium theatre, the third largest in the United States. Its interior decor was finished in soft ivory, blue, and gold, with life-size alabaster statues of the Muses set in niches above the box seats. A huge Japanese parasol-type dome stretched eighty feet above the main hall.

The three land sides of the park were enclosed by a high wooden fence, inside which flowed a moat. The stream was landscaped, with rustic bridges crossing it at intervals. Three thousand loads of California sand were hauled in to create a 500 foot sloping bathing beach.

By the first of June animals started arriving for the large menagerie building, which was 365 feet by 65 feet and located at the east end of the park, approximately where the present stone boathouse stands. There was a herd of African ostriches, four male and four female with eight young, which were trained to pull a Cinderella's Coach around the park, and who had a predilection for the magnificent artificial fruits and flowers which decorated the elaborate hats of the ladies. There were camels, lions, tigers, and at least 40 different species of animals shipped from New York. Buffalo, antelope, elk, and bear were brought from our own western plains and mountains. For the most part pairs were bought and the management announced that propagation would be practiced. A cable was received and highly publicized that a purchasing agent in Australia had secured a herd of kangaroos and a party of bushmen for Manhattan Beach, but there does not seem to be any record of their actually arriving.

Just two days before the scheduled formal opening of

An early view of
Manhattan Beach park

Manhattan Beach
Auditorium was the third
largest in the United States

the Beach, an unexpected bit of excitement occurred. Whether a fabricated publicity story or an actual happening, newspaper stories told of three sea lions which escaped their cage and took off for the lake. The keeper and manager, with telescopes, located two of the missing creatures, a mother and her calf, sunning on the deck of a boat at the water's edge. A park roustabout was summoned to lasso them. He succeeded in roping the mother, but the baby slid off into the water. After much struggling the mother escaped the rope and joined her baby. By noon twenty men had joined a sea lion hunt all over the land-locked lake. The male and the baby were captured, but the cow eluded them until they took the baby out in a boat and teased it. Its distress cries caused the mother to surface and be caught.

On opening day, June 27, 1891, 10,000 people jammed street cars, boats and wagons to visit Manhattan Beach. Mothers in long full skirts and mutton leg sleeves tried vainly to keep rein on fascinated little girls in white starched dresses and on boisterous boys dressed for the occasion in knee length trousers and blouses. Fathers, in their bowler hats, struggled with big picnic baskets and lemonade jugs. Excitement and noise were rampant.

Featured attractions for opening week were wrestling bears, a gypsy band, contortionists, the anti-gravity man who walked across ceilings — these in addition to the merry-go-round, ferris wheel, roller coaster, children's playground, and miles of promenades with inviting benches along the way. Balloon men, popcorn and peanut hawkers, clowns, and organ grinders all added to the merriment. A magnificent electric fountain from Paris tossed water seventy-five feet into the air with rainbow colors playing across it at night. The "new" *City of Denver*, the refurbished coal barge, made the rounds of the lake with a small band on board. In addition, a dance pavilion extended out over the water from the shore, and dance music swept over the lake from two bands there.

So much to see and do! Cavalry drills, bareback riding, spectacular fireworks displays, baseball games, a miniature railroad, fishing, boating. There were dog and pony acts, boxing matches, sideshow attractions such as the tallest woman in the world. Manhattan Beach seemed all boisterous carnival.

During the following summers numerous concessions drew a following. One, run by an Eskimo family, provided rides about the park in a dog sled mounted on wheels. When the family had a baby boy, much fanfare was given to his christening, the first Eskimo child born in the Denver area. Another popular concession was the Noll "buttermilk cow," a mechanical but very lifelike animal, from whose udders one could buy fresh milk or buttermilk.

And there were many chilling exhibitions of daring — balloon ascensions, parachute jumping, high wire acts, persons shot out of cannons. Marvelous Marsh was an intrepid actor who rode a bicycle down a 70 degree incline, 150 feet long, to plunge over the handlebars into a forty foot tank of water. One of these acts of derring-do turned into a tragedy. Or was it an advertising stunt? No one ever knew for sure. A young man, Ben Bowen, performed in an act where he was shot out of an imitation cannon suspended from a hot air balloon. This time the balloon, palely illuminated, drifted down into the center of the lake. Rescuers never found the body. His hat was found on the beach — that was all.

Another incident was more tragic. There was a large gentle elephant, named Roger, outfitted with a howdah, in which children rode about the park. One crowded Sunday afternoon a swaying balloon ascension frightened Roger and in panic he headed for his corral. A ten year old boy fell from the howdah and Roger stepped on his head. The other children clung to the sides until the animal was subdued.

In 1906 an electric tower was purchased from the St. Louis Fair and shipped to the park. One hundred ten feet tall, the steel structure had a passenger cage that spiraled around the tower to the top, moved by cogs. A three foot wide observation platform at the top permitted the visitor a bird's-eye view of the entire park and lake and a magnificent panoramic sight of the blue and white Rockies.

The theater was Manhattan Beach's biggest attraction. The specialty was musical comedy, and the great and the almost-great in that field performed, although the theater was so large that often the audience seemed of meager size. For a few seasons Mary Elitch-Long managed both the Elitch Gardens and the Manhattan Beach theaters.

The trip to Manhattan Beach from Denver was long. Cable cars furnished transportation across the railroad tracks to the car barns at Gallup Avenue (Zuni Street), and also over the Larimer Street trestle as far west on Colfax as present Utica Street, where the Glen Park Cottage stood, a sprawling shingle covered building with a many faceted roof and a broad verandah, which was a popular "rural" resort. There open air electric cars continued the trip on Sheridan Boulevard, along the west side of Sloan's Lake, to the gate of Manhattan Beach, to Elitch's, and on to the Berkeley Resort. In the winters the gaily filled streetcars continued to make their circle trip, bringing skaters to Sloan's Lake where the Manhattan Beach bands played waltzes, to which the warmly and brightly clad men and women glided by. The Satriano band played at Manhattan Beach many seasons.

At one point Manhattan Beach and Elitch Gardens sued to be allowed to withdraw from the city of Highlands, stating that they received little benefit from the taxes they paid. They were mollified by the city's promise to pipe water to the parks, and they withdrew their suit.

Another time Highlands sought to have a three mile limit declared for their boundaries, so that the town of Edgewater could not be a source of alcoholic drinks for Manhattan Beach patrons, but the suit was thrown out of court. The original Sloan's Lake Resort had been a beer garden, but when it became Manhattan Beach and was annexed by Highlands, of course the beer had to go. However the Beach was on the county line and, just across the road in Jefferson County, was what was then the rag-tag town of Edgewater. By knocking a few boards loose in the high wooden fence of the park, patrons could slip across the county line road where there were five saloons in one block, with cribs above, a German beer garden at the corner, and even a gambling table, reputed to be Soapy Smith's, in the middle of the intersection by the main gate to Manhattan Beach.

One wintry night, December 26, 1908, a watchman of the closed park chased off two boys who had been skating and who were trying to build a fire to keep warm. A few hours later people in Edgewater looked out in horror at the raging inferno that had been Manhattan Beach. Children sent upstairs to bed stood scraping frost off the windows to peer out at flames and sparks spurting up to turn the midnight sky crimson. Their fathers and brothers donned mackinaws and boots to help the little volunteer fire department establish a fire break at Sheridan Road so the devouring flames would not cross to engulf Edgewater.

Men and women from Edgewater, Lakewood, and Denver fought futilely to save their park. Fire horses reared and panicked. Men ran about shouting orders, hauling hoses, and forming bucket brigades. A south wind carried live sparks several blocks to the north. Glass windows in the buildings across the road buckled and shattered from the heat.

At dawn, when the smoke lifted off Sloan's Lake, most of Manhattan Beach was gone, buried beneath smouldering ashes. The beautiful theater was completely destroyed. Sparks had set fire to the dancing pavilion numerous times but the firemen had saved most of it and some adjoining buildings. The observation tower was damaged, and the west and north fences gone. The

The *Frolic* carried 1000 passengers and had two dance floors

menagerie building, with some of the animals in winter quarters elsewhere, had escaped.

There were whispers of arson. The watchman remembered the boys he had tried to chase home. Others remembered that sometimes tramps slipped into the grounds. No one will ever know the true story of the fire, but the owners viewed the wreckage and signed the death warrant of Manhattan Beach.

Nevertheless, shortly after the fire, negotiations were started for purchase of the property and what remained of the park. Albert Lewin, one of the founders of Lakeside Amusement Park not more than two miles from Sloan's Lake, was one of the developers of the new park. They named it Luna Park, but to Denverites it would always be Manhattan Beach, to which it seems but an epilogue.

The fifteen year lease held by Lewin and his associates included, besides the Manhattan Beach property, a little remembered four acre island in the southwest part of the lake, known as Hidalgo Island. At some time there was a dance hall on it and perhaps other buildings. The waters gradually ate away at the shores of the island and eventually it was necessary to join it to the mainland. For many years the Denver Municipal Trap Club occupied the spot, now part of Sloan's Park.

Luna Park was opened in the summer of 1909. The *City of Denver* had capsized in a storm. In 1910 a three deck sidewheeler, built at the lake, was launched. It had a capacity of almost 1000 passengers and boasted two fine dance floors on the decks. A contest was held by the *Rocky Mountain News* among the school children of the city for an appropriate name, and *Frolic* was selected. The *Frolic* was by far the most elaborate boat to sail the waters of Sloan's Lake and was the most popular attraction of Luna Park.

However, despite the allure of the *Frolic*, attendance at Luna Park dwindled. Various free attractions were offered — a free gate, free dancing, occasional free bronco busting shows, and vaudeville. There were even lunches at no charge, pony rides, free peanuts, and fortune tellers. Elitch Gardens and Lakeside both strongly competed for the clientele of Luna Park. The theater had been the greatest drawing card for Manhattan Beach and without it Luna Park lost its "respectable" patrons.

Its attraction for the sporting and rowdy elements contributed to Luna Park's decline. The saloons of Edgewater were very handy and, in spite of extra guards policing the area, there were increasing incidents of brawling, of loose boards in the fence, and of gate crashers. Dancers in the pavilion were pelted with garbage and whiskey bottles thrown from row boats on the lake, some returned by the dancers at the boaters, and fist fights were common. Slowly but surely, after twenty years of popularity, Manhattan Beach-Luna Park was deteriorating until "nice people" refused to go there.

Luna Park did not go out in excitement as did Manhattan Beach. Instead it simply seemed to die away. No mention is made in the newspapers after 1914. The animals were sold to City Park Zoo. The *Frolic* was dismantled at the lake. A world war came along and building materials were scarce. Luna Park seemed to be a good source of spare lumber. By the 1920's Sloan's Lake had again reverted to swamp and cattails, a habitat for blackbirds, ducks, and geese.

The city government of Denver in 1906 and again in 1936 bought pieces of the property around the lake. Cultivation into a city park was started in the 1930's, partly as a WPA project. For many years a few blackened piles stood in the water at the edge of the lake, but they, too, disappeared. For the water skiers, boaters, fishermen, and picnickers who now keep the park and lake busy, it is hard to believe that a magnificent amusement park once stood in the triangle between Sheridan, West Byron Place, and Wolff Street.

Rivalry of Denver and Highlands

In 1890 Highlands was riding the top of the crest of success and affluence. Denver had tried many times to annex Highlands, but Highlands always voted it down. They did not want to be part of the big dirty sinful city.

Instead, they set about to build their own city hall. City offices had been, first, in a store front building at 2749 West 25th Avenue, and later, in the Arbuckle Building. Now they built a handsome three story brick and sandstone City Hall, designed by William Quayle, at the southwest corner of Highland Avenue (now West 26th) and the Boulevard (Federal). This was the geographic center of the town. The building had stores on the ground floor, a drug store in the corner, the post office, the jail — even though they had little use for a jail for Highlands citizens. There is a story of two twelve year old girls who were incarcerated for a few hours for quarreling! Sometimes a peddler wandered across Zuni from North Denver, not realizing he was in a different town, and was fined $5 for not having a license. If he could not produce the money, he was clapped into jail.

The second floor had a large room used by various elegant dancing clubs, lodges and churches without their own buildings. It was topped by an imposing square corner tower.

At the dedication of the City Hall, hostility between Denver and Highlands came out into the open. With the mayor of Denver, Wolfe Londoner, as a supposedly honored platform guest, Mayor Lewis of Highlands said that people of Denver would be only too glad to live in Highlands if they could, where the people were more intelligent and the city government more capable than any other city in the state. The souvenir brochure of the occasion boasted that Highlands had electricity, street

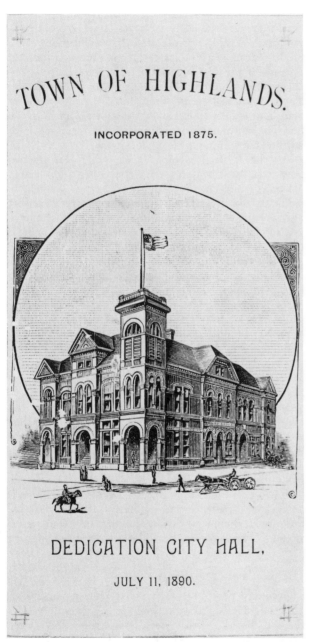

TOWN OF HIGHLANDS.

INCORPORATED 1875.

DEDICATION CITY HALL.

JULY 11, 1890.

Denver Public Library, Western History Department

Highlands City Hall

lights, telephones, thirty miles of sidewalks, streets "in better condition than the streets of any city of the state," a sewer system "much better than Denver's." They bragged that in a period of two years they had had no arrests for drunkenness or disturbance. They added, "There is not a pauper, a house of ill fame, or a saloon within the city." This was at a time when Denver's red light district was known from coast to coast.

Highlands predicted that in the next decade or two the entire territory stretching to the foot of the Rockies would be embraced within the city of Highlands, with a population of 300,000, all of whom would transact the daily business of earning a living in Denver and then return at night to their genteel bedrooms in the quiet clean atmosphere of Highlands for "rest, refreshment and family comfort."

Denver's mayor did not take this meekly. He was angry and said that Highlands had less crime than Denver because it was much easier to govern a city of 8,000 than one of 130,000. Then he dropped the bomb. He declared that the only way Highlands would get an increase in population was not by spreading to the foothills but by coming into Denver. "I wouldn't have said a word if your mayor had not pitched into me, but unless you annex yourself to Denver, I don't see how you can get the viaduct you want!"

And thus Highlands' day of triumph turned into a doomsday. Adequate transportation into Denver had always been· Highlands', as well as North Denver's, biggest problem. The cable and electric line trestles at 16th Street and at Larimer Street were dangerous for teams and wagons or buggies. General Woodbury, at the dedication, said, "Railroads had all crossed the only streets that had been opened between the north and east divisions in Denver." In addition, mass transportation was difficult. Highlands had two electric lines and a steam motor line which connected with the city cable lines, but there it was necessary to pay another fare. The steam motor line, supposedly noiseless, had caused Highlanders distress because it was not noiseless, and it sometimes exceeded the speed limit of twelve miles an hour.

Highlands had already experienced a blow through the lack of a viaduct. St. Luke's Hospital in 1881 purchased the old Grandview Hotel at 17th and Federal. In

1883 there was a typhoid epidemic in the city and doctors, understandably, objected to driving the muddy and hazardous river bottoms at night to reach the hospital. The board of St. Luke's decided to move to 19th and Pearl, where they are today. Later this old hotel-hospital building burned.

The lack of a viaduct was the cause of many problems. A number of wealthy men of Highlands gave up and moved to the new fashionable district of Capitol Hill. Among these was Owen LeFevre, who had a home on the Boulevard and had served Highlands both as city attorney and as mayor. He, his wife, and talented daughter, who became Mrs. Harry Bellamy, are remembered as prominent leaders of Denver's society and philanthropic organizations.

And then another blow hit not only Highlands but all of Colorado. The Silver Panic of 1893! It was felt all over the country, but especially in the silver producing states of the west. Most of the paying mines in Colorado were rich in the white metal. Almost overnight these mines shut down, smelters closed, thousands of men were out of work. The depression snowballed, of course, throwing people in all businesses and trades into the same slough. Many men of Highlands, who had depended so heavily on mining or the merchandising influenced by mining, lost their wealth. Among the twelve banks in Denver that closed in 1893 was the North Denver Bank, headed by Silas S. Kennedy, but it managed to pay off its accounts in full before collapsing. General Woodbury lost his fortune and his lovely mansion, although it was always known by his name until it was torn down. This was the same time when John Brisben Walker's River Front Park was taken over by Coxey's army as an assembly camp.

The town government of Highlands also was a victim of the Panic. They had tried to build a Utopia. Now they found that, without the dirty industries they hated, a city of discreet homes could not pay for sewers, water, police and fire protection. The wooden sidewalks, of which they had bragged so recently, were rotting. The streets were ungravelled, often impassable after hard rains or in winter storms, and in summer boot-top high in dust. Sewers had become inadequate. The city was in debt.

Highlands had been proud of its volunteer fire de-partments with their two hose carts and strong horses. Now they were not adequate to take care of the sprawling town. A story was reported that when there was a fire in a store near Elitch's both carts were sent out, but because of the bad streets the volunteers became discouraged and turned back, simply letting the store burn down. Another time the firemen took streetcars to the blaze and let the horses plow through the mud to the fire. The mayor complained that the fire department was nothing but a dress parade organization.

Another frustrating point of jealousy between the two cities was the fact that Denver had door-to-door mail delivery, while Highlands did not. Senator Wolcott of Colorado was trying to change the federal ruling that only towns of 10,000 or more population might have this service, but at the time Highlands, with a population of 8,000, was excluded. People had to make the long trip to the post office in the City Hall, either by walking, riding " the cars," or hitching up the horse and buggy. It was a good two miles from the outlying districts. Some of the men had their mail delivered to their places of business in Denver, and their wives could only hope they would remember to bring it home.

But still Highlands voted against annexation. In 1894 the women of Colorado had been given their franchise to vote, and the ladies of Highlands voted down annexation two to one on the question of liquor and saloons.

Sometime and somehow in the next two years, the Highlands people were convinced by Denver that if they would only annex they could keep their $5,000 liquor license fee, and it could be changed only by a petition and vote of the people in the corporate limits of Highlands.

And so, on June 22, 1896, the taxpayers of Highlands voted over two to one to be annexed to Denver. Interestingly, there were no liquor outlets in the area until after 1933 when national prohibition was repealed.

Highlands after annexation

Becoming part of Denver was not a magic panacea for all of Highlands' problems. Perhaps Denver still wanted them to bleed a little, even though their knees were bent and their spirits badly bruised. The *Daily News* was especially vindictive with an item of November 18,

One of the two Highlands' fire carts

1896 headlined: "Debt Ridden Highlands. Special levy to defray the cost of boodling." It went on to say, "When no longer able to keep the municipal ship afloat, North side gangsters unloaded all their stealings on an obliging neighbor." A kinder *Denver Times,* June 23, 1896, called it "the beautiful little suburb and village of Highlands . . . Denver, as a result of the action of Highlands taxpayers, is the gainer of 10,000 additional population, two square miles of the city upon which are built splendid homes, owned by actual residents, and broad well-lighted streets, many costly public buildings, every facility for transportation and internal improvements superior to many portions of the city."

The improvements for which Highlanders yearned the most were slow in coming. It was not until three years after annexation that the long-awaited 14th Street viaduct (now Speer viaduct) was completed. It was another ten years before the 20th Street viaduct, paid for mostly by residents of the northwest sector, was built. While better police and fire protection had been

Highlands fire station after annexation

one of the big reasons for annexation, Denver decided the fire protection provided by the four members of the fire department of Highlands would be adequate. Police protection was not much better. The handsome City Hall, its bell tower gone, was used for a while by overflow classes from Boulevard School, and then, the brick covered with stucco, for a fire and police department until 1966 when it was razed. A new fire station now stands on the same spot.

Denver for many years had been trying to straghten out its street names. Now they also changed those west of Zuni, listing them alphabetically, with just enough streets to go from Alcott to Zenobia. The east-west avenues were changed to numbers to correspond to those in east Denver.

Highlands continued as a residential section of the city with — almost — no industry to sully its pure air. However, for some twenty years there was a disturbing scent in the elite atmosphere. Ordinarily when the circus comes to town, it means a fun time; but when the circus came to old Highlands, it was an unhappy occasion, for it came to stay. The circus was the Sells-Floto,

E. E. Stanchfield

Sells Floto Circus used the old stove foundry for winter quarters

one of the *Denver Post's* owners' playthings. In 1906 Harry H. Tammen and Frederick G. Bonfils secured property on the former S. S. Kennedy farm, which by now included a small stove foundry started by Kennedy's son-in-law, E. E. Stanchfield. The circus was headquartered in the winters in the foundry building and in barns established about it near West 26th Avenue and Indiana Street (now Hazel Court). Here the elephants trumpeted and the nocturnal big cats roared, spoiling the quiet nights of the neighborhood. The many animals fouled the air and the ground as well as the quiet. And they brought rats. But the animals were a delight to the children of the whole city.

On Sunday afternoons, the animal yard was open to the public, for a small admission price, and Denverites rode the streetcar out West 29th Avenue to the grounds, where they could see animals and other wonders of the circus world. There were an emu, eighteen elephants, camels, giraffes, monkeys, lions, tigers — all in open cages to be observed closely. New animal babies born during the winter had irresistible appeal for crowds of children, and the *Post* always announced when these new additions arrived.

After 1914 the main attraction was Buffalo Bill Cody,

an ill old man, who had gone through much bewildering litigation, had lost his famous Wild West Show, and found himself deeply in debt to Bonfils and Tammen. Dressed in his famous white buckskin suit, this old shadow of the former handsome idol spent Sunday afternoons putting on marksmanship shows, shooting glass balls filled with smoke. There was smoke but no longer any fire in his showmanship.

The elephants were kept busy, practicing putting up and taking down the big tent, and doing other heavy labor about the quarters. They were put to work in an unusual way during what will always be called "Denver's Big Snow of 1913." St. Clara's Orphanage, at West 29th Avenue and Newton Street, had run out of coal. With their usual knightly posture of rushing to the rescue, the *Post* publishers sent wagonloads of coal to the orphanage from another of their pet projects, the Denver Post Coal Company. Struggling up West 26th Avenue opposite the circus grounds, the coal teams foundered in the deep drifts. The wagons would not move. The frustrated drivers plowed through the waist high snow to the circus and got permission to use elephants. These mammoth animals trumpeted and bellowed at the cold wet drifts about their tropics-bred knees, but, one behind each wagon,

A beautifully restored Victorian home

they put their trunks around the rear axles, lifting the wagons off the ground. Rearing and plunging, the horses had to pull or be run over by their own wagons. St. Clara's received their coal and the orphans were saved from the cold.

William F. Cody died in 1917. The Sells Floto winter quarters remained in the center of old Highlands until 1920 when, because of Tammen's ill health, it was sold to a syndicate and winter quarters were moved to Peru, Indiana. The empty buildings stood, however, a haven for rats and mice, until 1939 when the neighbors insisted they be razed.

With annexation Highlands had experienced a traumatic transition, but it was not a fatal one. Some wealthy families continued to stay in the homes they loved, and stayed through successive generations. The corner groceries gave way to supermarkets; livery stables and feed and coal stores became garages or television repair shops. Little business blocks, built on corners along the streetcar lines, continued to stand, occupied by a succession of various small businesses. When streetcars were replaced by buses, they followed the same routes as the ones of the tracks.

In Highlands home building had been spotty, with some estates occupying a whole block, other blocks fully built up and nearby ones vacant. As these filled, this section of town became a good example of the types of middle class architecture in Denver. During the 1880's and '90's, some developers had built rows of five or six Victorian one story, or sometimes two story, houses in a block and left the rest vacant. These first were built on the narrow twenty-five foot lots allowed at that time. Later there were rows of Denver squares, of one story neo-classic, of so-called Anglo-Bengal bungalows with wide front porches which were built in the 1920's. Just before World War II the preferred style was English Tudor, large or small. After the war building was rapid and city lot size ranch houses were built. Then suddenly there were very few lots left on which to build, and this part of Northwest Denver became static.

In just the last few years Highlands has been rediscovered as the last bit of early Denver with a great many undeteriorated houses. Young couples are buying houses to restore them to their Victorian glory, to go along with those that have been kept in good condition by loving families.

That early pride of Highlanders has never died. The people are still proud of their homes, their gardens, their trees, their churches, their schools. They are proud of their pure cold water, which they swear is colder than that in any other part of Denver. They are proud of their pure air, perhaps not so unsullied as at one time, but above most of the city's smog, so that they still have their treasured view of the towering blue and white sentinels of the Rockies, and, with a man of the 1890's, they can "look down from their happy homes on the eminence where Highlands proudly sits, upon the smoky city below."

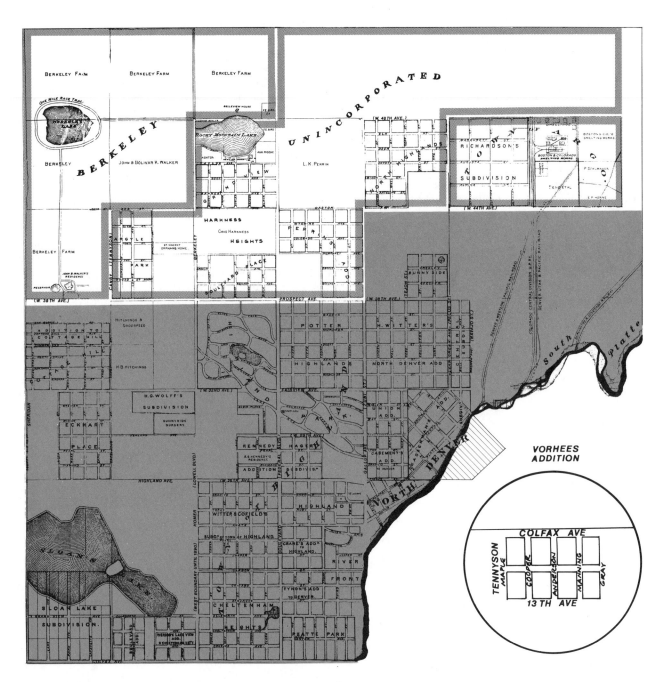

BERKELEY FARM · BERKELEY FARM · BERKELEY FARM

UNINCORPORATED

One Mile Race Trac.

BERKELEY

BERKELEY

BERKELEY FARM

JOHN & BOLIVAR K. WALKER

ROCKY MOUNTAIN LAKE

L. K. PERRIN

RICHARDSON'S SUBDIVISION

BOSTON & COLO SMELTING WORKS

BOSTON & COLORADO SMELTING WORKS

P. SCHUMAKER

E. P. HONNE

(W. 48TH AVE.)

(W. 44TH AVE.)

ROCKY HIGHLANDS

HARKNESS HEIGHTS

Chas Harkness

PERRY'S 2ND ADD

ST. VINCENT ORPHANS HOME

ARGYLE PARK

BOULEVARD PLACE

PROSPECT AVE.

(W. 38TH AVE.)

CANBY (TENNYSON)

BUNNY SIDE

HITCHINGS & GOODSPEED

POTTER HIGHLANDS

H. WITTER'S

NORTH DENVER ADD.

ADDITION TO COTTAGE HILL

H. B. HITCHINGS

H. G. WOLFF'S SUBDIVISION

SUNNYSIDE NURSERY

FAIRVIEW AVE.

UNION ADD.

ECKHART PLACE

SHERIDAN

(W. 32ND AVE.)

KENNEDY HAGERTY

S. S. KENNEDY'S RESIDENCE

ADDITION SUBDIV'N

CASEMENT'S ADD

NORTH DENVER

HIGHLAND AVE.

HIGHLAND

(LOWELL BLVD.)

(W. 26TH AVE.)

WITTER & COFIELD'S

SUBD'S OF TOWN OF HIGHLAND

CRANE'S ADD'N TO HIGHLAND

RIVER

FRONT

South Platte

VORHEES ADDITION

SLOAN'S LAKE

TYRON'S ADD TO DENVER

CHELTENHAM

HEIGHTS

PLATTE PARK

SLOAN LAKE SUBDIVISION.

CHELTENHAM H'TS

COLFAX AVE

TENNYSON · MAPLE · COOPER · ANDERSON · MANNING · GRAY

13TH AVE

154

Towns on the Perimeter

West Colfax

A miniscule distinguished development across Colfax Avenue from Highlands must be included in this story, although — since it is on the south side of West Colfax Avenue — it is not, in the strict sense, a part of Northwest Denver. It consists only of both sides of one block on one street — both sides of Stuart Street from the southeast and southwest corners of 14th Avenue to a little south of Colfax.

This one block was part of a small real estate development, extending from (now) Perry Street on the east to (now) Tennyson Street on the west, a matter of four blocks, and only two blocks wide, from West 13th Avenue to West Colfax Avenue. The subdivision was established by Ralph Voorhees, who considered this area the perfect spot for pure air and an excellent view of the mountains, the two assets dearly desired by all early day Denverites.

After the rough frontier days were over, the west, with its triple promise of health, wealth, and opportunity, drew hundreds of young men from the more crowded cities of the east coast. Ralph Voorhees was one of these men. He came from New York in 1872 and served first as a ticket agent for the newborn Denver & Rio Grande Railroad. He was quite an athlete and held the record in New York for the 800 yard dash. When he arrived in Denver, he joined the volunteer fire department, and was a welcome member in those days when the men pulled the carts, and speed and strength were essential.

When there were no fires, one of the exciting entertainments of the day was races between the various hose companies.

Voorhees married in 1885, and he and Mrs. Voorhees had four children. He became a very successful real estate man and was a member of the Colorado legislature. In this capacity he introduced a bill to establish Flag Day in Colorado on June 14th, and became dubbed the father of Flag Day. He was one of the founders of Colorado Woman's College. In large part he financed the building of the West Colfax, or Larimer Street, trestle, so that west section of the Denver suburbs might have cable car service.

In 1891 Voorhees plotted the lots for the West Colfax subdivision. This had been an undeveloped part of the town of Colfax, which sprouted on the west bank of the Platte and continued in a narrow strip along West Colfax Avenue to the county line of Sheridan Boulevard. As the years passed, the Jewish immigrants, who had first settled in Auraria, spread farther and farther west on both sides of Colfax Avenue, with their little businesses — which grew into big businesses — their homes, schools, and synagogues. From the 1920's to the 1950's, the area was largely Jewish. Characteristic of other Northwest Denver neighborhoods, families who had previously lived in the scattered homes and small farms south of Sloan's Lake stayed to contribute to the ethnic and cultural blend, as did the affluent families of the Voorhees subdivision.

Courtesy of Star Bread Company

A West Colfax business which grew from two wagons to 101 motorized units

Voorhees built seven houses in the area. His own home, at 1471 Stuart Street, designed by Lang and Pugh, was a luxurious stone palace, which has been kept in excellent condition by the two or three families who have occupied it. *The Western Architect and Building News* of January, 1890, described it as of hand hewn lava, finished throughout with beautiful woods, with the main hall of quarter sawed oak, carved and panelled; the parlor and library of cherry; dining room of Georgia curled pine; pantries and kitchen of Texas pine. The second and third floors are of black ash and Georgia curly pine. It had a third floor wrought iron balcony, where the family gathered to watch the exciting fireworks displays at the amusement parks.

Another three story house just south of the Voorhees', with adjoining gardens, is of rusticated stone, designed more like a church than a residence, with a square tower with open cupola on the north side, and five ascending narrow stained glass windows along the stairway on the south. This home for many years was

Berkeley-Lainson

Voorhees home south of West Colfax

occupied by the Frank I. Smith family, with six zestful children. One of the sons, Paul, married Ferne Whiteman, who was a fine vocalist and sister of Paul Whiteman, the jazz king who grew up in Denver.

One home which Voorhees built, which has since been razed, was at the southeast corner of West Colfax and Stuart, the residence of F. W. White, courtly drama writer for the *Denver Post* for many years, who always signed his columns as "F.W.W." His son Frank followed his father on the staff of the *Post*. F.W.W.'s daughter, Lillian White Spencer, was a distinguished and nationally known poet and librettist, and an authority on

157

The Smith residence
south of Voorhees

The widow of one of Denver's early sheriffs also lived in West Colfax

Dr. Gerald Bliss, a member of the honor guard at Lincoln's casket, lived here nearly fifty years

Another of the homes in the West Colfax section

Indian lore. She also made her home here for many years.

Another large stone and shingle house at 1444 Stuart Street was occupied by the widow of Mike Spangler. Spangler had been sheriff of huge Arapahoe County, a county that was part rural, part urban, part staid and morally upright, part wide open to all the ruffians and scoundrels of the west. He was elected in 1879 and re-elected at the end of his term, and during that time he encountered con men who seemed to run rampant over the west, murderers, gamblers, prostitutes, thieves, and pimps. Probably one of the most exciting incidents of his career occurred when an erroneous rumor spread over Denver that a Chinaman had murdered a white man. Bigotry was strong against the Chinese of the town, and immediately a mob gathered. They chased the terrified residents of the Chinatown of Denver, hanged one defenseless old man, and resisted a fire hose turned on them by police. When Sheriff Spangler and his deputies, with a former sheriff, approached the mob unafraid, they at last recognized authority and began to break up. The leaders were arrested and by ten o'clock that night the riot was over.

Following his terms as sheriff, Mike Spangler became vice president of the Union National Bank, and he and his wife had an elegant home at 10th and Pennsylvania. Mrs. Spangler, as a widow, moved to the West Colfax and Stuart residence to be near her sister, who was Mrs. Ralph Voorhees.

Two houses of this prestigious suburb, facing each other across Stuart Street, on the south side of 14th Avenue, are of brick and shingle construction, with steeply inclined roofs and tiny intriguing dormers and balconies. The one at 1389 Stuart Street was occupied by Dr. Gerald Bliss and his second wife for all of their married life, both dying in 1945. Dr. Bliss was a Civil War veteran and had been a member of the honor guard over Lincoln's casket. He had gone to South Dakota where he practiced medicine for many years before retiring and moving to Colorado. He lived nearly fifty years after his retirement and was 99 years old when he died.

All of these four West Colfax houses have been designated as official landmarks.

At the southeast corner, opposite the Bliss home, is a three story house, at 1390 Stuart. It has a very steep pitched roof, bay window, and balcony. For many years this was the home of Miss Elizabeth McNulty, a teacher at nearby Glen Park School, and her two aunts. At another time it was the home of Roady Kenehan, a hearty Irishman who was active in Colorado politics and served as State Treasurer and Auditor.

The town of Colfax, including this exclusive little section with its big homes, was annexed to Denver in 1895, but the fine homes, surrounded now by smaller ones, remain as a tribute to Ralph Voorhees.

Argo

"Why is the #5 bus line called Argo, and what or where is Argo?" is a legitimate question today, for this bus line name is about all that is retained of the once busy smelter town of Argo, located at the very northeast corner of northwest Denver, bounded by (now) Pecos Street on the west, Broadway on the east, West 44th Avenue on the south, and West 48th Avenue on the north. It was built around the Argo smelter of the Boston and Colorado Smelting Company, founded by Nathaniel P. Hill, a familiar name in Colorado mining and social history. Mr. Hill, formerly a professor of chemistry at Brown University, had developed a process of extracting gold from ore which was much simpler and more usable than any other method then known. In 1867 he started a smelter at Black Hawk. His process revitalized mining in Colorado, but the canyon in which Black Hawk is located soon was too cramped to allow for expansion of the smelter, and in 1878 the plant was moved to the Argo location two miles north and west of what was then the center of Denver.

Argo was incorporated as a village in 1879 by an election of the residents, most of whom were smelter workers. Later trainmen employed by the Moffat Railroad, which had its roundhouse and shops not too far to the north, also lived in Argo. The town was fairly well built up with homes and small stores.

Almost all the residents were immigrant families, the large part of them Swedish, with a smattering of Germans, Scotch, Poles, Hungarians, and Slavs. These people came to Colorado, as did other immigrant groups, to obtain more opportunity for themselves, escape compulsory military proscription — which pro-

Boston and Colorado Smelter at Argo

vided no compensation for dependents, and to give their children a chance at that American ideal of life, liberty and the pursuit of happiness. Still, how much liberty did these men really gain for themselves? They worked long days of twelve hours, seven days a week, with no holidays or vacation, at a wage of $2.25 a day. Safety precautions were non-existent in the smelters, and men tied damp rags or burlap sacks around their noses and mouths to keep out the fine infiltrating dust. Neverthe-

less, many died of "miner's consumption," as silicosis was called.

It was necessary for everyone in the family to work to bring in enough money to make a frugal living. The wives, besides caring for their own families, took in boarders, which meant doing their laundry as well as providing board and room. Others took in laundry, and one of these specialized in washing and stretching lace curtains, inevitable in every home in the city, a business

Horse car climbing a hill towards Argo

which developed into a large lace and fine linens laundry, which is still doing business today. In this instance, a cement floored room was added to their own large house as a curtain drying room, which also served wonderfully as a roller skating rink for the children. Other wives and daughters went out to work in the wealthier homes in the more affluent parts of Denver. Many were fine cooks, caterers, or bakers. And at home they kept their tidy houses, lawns, vegetable and flower gardens, and raised chickens as a sideline.

There was a hotel in Argo, a train stop at the Junction, and a horse car line which ran from Denver across the prairies between the scattered houses of North Denver and Argo. In 1898 the Argo residents protested the poor and slow service provided by the two dingy horse cars. Whether it was improved is not known, but the present bus line follows very much the route of the old horse car line that went up Pecos to 38th and then up Lipan to 48th.

An elementary school, which taught first through sixth grades, was north of the smelter and across the railroad tracks. The children trudged the frozen rutted dirt streets for almost a mile, and the more adventuresome crawled under trains — with some tragic results — in order not to be late for school. Denver downtown churches conducted missions in Argo, some having their own small buildings where, once a week, usually midweek, the minister would hold services and teach catechisms. As a startling reminder of what the section used to be, at West 44th and Jason, amid the warehouses and railroad tracks, sits a small weather-beaten, once-white frame church, its gothic windows boarded, its door nailed shut. It was originally the Argo Methodist Episcopal Church.

The various nationalities lived in their own small neighborhoods. Inca Street was always known as Småland Avenue, because all the residents came from Småland, a part of Sweden. Here they could be at home in their familiar language, eat their delicious native dishes, hold their *kaffe kalas,* and in the men's few free hours at home they could enjoy their beer, music, and companionship.

When Denver was made into a separate county in 1902 by the state legislature, the north boundary was a mid-section line which became West 52nd Avenue. All the property below that automatically became part of Denver, and thus Argo was swallowed up. The last meeting of the Argo board of trustees was held May 8, 1903, at which they incorporated into Denver, with a balance of one cent in their treasury. At least they were sure Denver would not get rich from the acquisition. The smelter burned in 1913 and was not rebuilt. The little Argo school property was returned by the Denver school district to the Nathaniel P. Hill estate in 1916 and torn down about 1925.

By that time Argo families had grown up. Although with a nostalgic feeling for their childhood homes, they moved to other parts of the city, away from the railroad tracks. Fulfilling their fathers' dreams, they had developed into fine mechanics, craftsmen, engineers, teachers, and businessmen. A large part of the area today is occupied by a major public housing facility, opened in 1952. A few of the old houses still cling to the land here and there, but most of the rest of Argo has been cut by superhighways, railroads, and industries, until it is hard today to realize that at one time this was a quiet residential neighborhood.

Bob Bond

The weatherbeaten Argo Methodist Church

Berkeley

About two miles north of the junction of Cherry Creek and the South Platte River runs a long high ridge. It was this ridge that very early travelers followed as they left the hamlet of Denver, stopping at the water hole that is now Rocky Mountain Lake at West 47th and Federal, and traveling on toward Boulder Diggings or Wyoming.

The trail dipped down to Clear Creek at Jim Baker's Crossing. Jim, a gaunt man with luxuriant golden curls, had roamed the Rocky Mountains for years, as a hunter, trapper, trader, a trusted guide and scout for General John C. Fremont, who made five government and surveying expeditions to the Rockies. Baker was one of the best known of the frontier men, along with his friends, Jim Bridger, Kit Carson, Dick Wooten, Oliver Wiggins. Jim Baker finally settled on the south bank of Clear Creek and built an adobe store and home for his Shoshone wife and children a little west of what is now Tennyson Street. He operated a ferry where all travelers to the north crossed the turbulent creek. Later he built a toll bridge. He received a United States grant to 160 acres along the south side of the creek, enjoyed his family and managed the little store, where he sold supplies such as hay, flour, and whiskey, to the few travelers who came his way. After the death of a daughter, which grieved him greatly, he left the turmoil of this civilization for a secluded ranch on the Snake River, just south of the Colorado-Wyoming line in northwest Colorado. There he died in 1898. Later deeds to the quarter section that had been Baker's along Clear Creek exempted a small cemetery site, but in very recent years, when the steep slope of the ridge was being bulldozed for a mobile home park, the graves of, probably, the wife and children of Jim Baker's were unearthed.

Adjoining Baker's quarter section on the south and over the ridge of the hill was another homestead grant, this one to Washington Hepner in 1863. There is little known about Hepner. Perhaps he was the proprietor of a dance hall called Hepner's Gardens in Denver. A choice bit of journalism in the *Rocky Mountain News* of August 22, 1863, told about these "Gardens," saying that "A fraction of Denver's queenly, charming carmine [sic], pretty, polished, paragons of grandeur, grace and gentleness adorned the ballroom floor from ten to three."

Hepner must not have developed his quarter section, for a homestead grant is shown to John Hughes from the United States in 1870. Hughes is better recorded. He was a Welshman who came to Colorado in 1865, and was in the charcoal business and in freighting. But in 1870, apparently shortly after he bought the farm, he and his brother moved to Pueblo, and this left the farm for sale again.

John Brisben Walker, who never ran out of ways to make money, became the owner in 1879. Soon after he came to Denver, in addition to superintending the Scotch-named subdivision of Highland Park, he saw the possibilities of alfalfa as the coming agricultural product in Colorado. He bought the farm on the south slope of the ridge, added to it, until he had 1600-1700 acres, which he named Berkeley Farm, possibly for Berkeley Springs, Virginia, where he and his wife had lived, and where his son, John Brisben Walker, Jr., was born. Walker and Dr. William A. Bell, the Londoner who invested so heavily in the west, formed the Berkeley Farm and Cattle Company, in 1885, to handle the farm.

There was a swampy lake below the ridge, which was developed as a reservoir by the Rocky Mountain Ditch Company and known as Berkeley Lake. On an 1885 map by Edward Rollandet, a mile long race track is shown circling the lake. Walker built his home still farther south, just off Prospect Avenue (now West 38th Avenue), at what is today Winona Court, a street which was not cut through at that time. On maps the house, which has been razed, is shown with a long circular driveway and with a reservoir near the house.

The extensive Berkeley farm was a very successful alfalfa project, but Walker was anxious to plunge into new fields and new money making ventures. He gave fifty acres of his farm to the Jesuit College, which had been located in Morrison, to be used as a campus on the hills south of Clear Creek, at now Lowell Boulevard. The Sacred Heart College moved there in 1887 and in 1921 became Regis College. In 1888 Walker sold the rest of his farm. He had bought it for $1,000; he sold it for $325,000. The new purchasers were a Kansas City syndicate, who put the real estate and investment firm of Carleton Ellis and John McDonough in charge of the development of a new suburb here. Immediately William Lang, a prominent and popular architect of that period in Denver, was commissioned to design thirty-five houses for the Berkeley area. Although not as elaborate as the Capitol Hill houses he designed, some fifteen to twenty houses still remaining in Berkeley bear strong similarity to the house Lang designed for Carleton Ellis in Highlands. They are of brick and shingle construction and show floor plans, small roof line windows, second story porches, and exciting tower details, all typical of Lang design. A group of these is situated on Wolff Street, just north of 38th Avenue and others are scattered about Berkeley Hill.

Bob Bond

A Berkeley house in Lang style

Frank Leslie's Illustrated, a popular national newspaper, in its September, 1889 issue, reported: "Berkeley contains more than 1700 acres, including a park of 160 acres and college grounds of 50 acres. There is no more healthful spot anywhere, without the dust, smoke, and odors of the city. There is abundant water, pure air, and rich soil. There is a superior water system. Long known as the finest alfalfa field in Colorado, its innumerable ditches and abundant water are no less useful to the owner of a home with spacious grounds. The owners have substituted miles of iron pipes for ditches. There are cable and motor lines. Many trees have been set out

Berkeley Lake today, showing the tower of Lakeside Amusement Park, just across the city limits

in the park this year. No intoxicating liquors are sold in the suburb." Despite this glowing prospectus, the new suburb did not build up rapidly. Houses were scattered, streets were ungraded and unsurfaced. There were no curbs and few sidewalks.

The developers, Ellis and McDonough, did not live in Berkeley. In 1890 Carleton Ellis had William Lang design a house for him in Highlands, at (now) West 30th Avenue and Lowell Boulevard. Ellis' Denver story is elusive. During the few years between 1889 and 1895 he was active in investments and real estate and was vice-president of the Citizens Savings Bank, one of the many

Denver banks which closed its doors in the Panic of 1893, although the bank did pay its depositors in full and was reorganized. Mr. Ellis is mentioned in Smiley's *History of Denver* as one of the members, in 1895, of the board of directors of the newly organized Festival of the Mountain and Plain, a gala affair which was repeated in Denver for several years. In 1897 Mrs. Carleton Ellis was listed in the city directory at an address in Berkeley, at the corner of (now) West 39th Avenue and Wolff Street, a red brick square house. The only other available information on the family is a burial permit for a Carleton Ellis, age five years, who died of scarletina, listed from this Berkeley address in 1901.

John McDonough is a much better documented person. He did not live in Berkeley but near a later development of his, Harkness Heights, where his large home stands and is described in the section covering this development.

In 1892 on the petition of 41 residents, a town was incorporated under the name of "The Town of North Denver," with 450 inhabitants. Its boundaries were the same as the boundaries of John Brisben Walker's Berkeley farm, which, by today's street names, were: West 52nd Avenue on the north, Sheridan Boulevard on the west, and the east and south boundaries stair-stepping from 38th and Sheridan to Tennyson, Tennyson from 38th to 44th, 44th Avenue from Tennyson to Perry, Perry from 44th to 48th, 48th Avenue from Perry to Federal, and Federal to 52nd.

The new town officials, meeting in the Berkeley post office building, at the southeast corner of West 45th and Yates Street, set about immediately organizing committees and passing ordinances to solve various problems. They had a $1,000 retail liquor license fee. They required a $10 license for a billiard table, a bowling alley, bagatelle (a game played on a board which had holes in one end into which balls were struck with a cue), pigeonhole (a betting game for which the author cannot find a description), ten pin alleys. There were to be no cock fights, dog fights, or prize fights. There was a $50 fine for being drunk. No horses, cattle, swine, sheep, goats, or geese were to run at large, which indicates that the Town of North Denver was much more rural than urban.

One of the confusing things about the Town of North Denver was its street names. Streets were true to the compass, but the town council could not keep its mind made up about the names. They called the north-south streets by tree names and the east-west by numbers. Later the whole thing was reversed, giving the tree names to the east-west and the numbers to the north-south. They also experimented with letters of the alphabet. A researcher has quite a puzzle on his hands when he tries today to locate one of the old addresses.

In 1896 the Town of North Denver found itself in an embarrassing situation. The unincorporated areas east of the town had been annexed by Denver in 1893, and Highlands, directly to the south, in 1896. Consequently, the Town of North Denver was surrounded by North Denver. As a result, in 1898 the town council changed the town's name to Berkeley, which had been the name of the post office since it was established in 1890, and in whose building the town offices were located. However, by this time the post office name had been changed to Alcott and moved to 41st and Tennyson. Nevertheless, the town name remained Berkeley, with their offices in the building at 45th and Yates, the park and lake are Berkeley, and the bus line is still called Berkeley.

Domestic water was piped into Berkeley by the Beaver Brook Water Company, and also by the Denver Union Water Company. Here, as in Highlands, artesian water was easily found; in fact, a large area along Prospect Avenue was swampy and muddy from underground water. There was an artesian well, 640 feet deep, at West 38th and Tennyson, and another at West 43rd and Zenobia. Most Berkeley residents had their own backyard wells with hand pumps or windmills, and many of the houses were without indoor plumbing, except possibly a pump at the kitchen sink. At the back of the lot there would be a privy discreetly hidden by lilac and hollyhocks.

There was no industry in Berkeley. Commerce was confined to the corner grocery or drug store, the coal, feed and ice company. In the early days there were at least two livery stables, and one day excitement rocked the neighborhood around one of them. The livery stable had been held up! Two cowboys made the owner, at gun point, feed their horses and demanded booty — of one bag of feed. After the post office was moved to 41st and

Original Berkeley Post Office and City Hall

Denver Public Schools

Louisa M. Alcott School

Tennyson in 1896, a business area grew up there, with a dry goods store which became the first of a presently large chain (Eaker's), an early movie theater, drug, hardware, and furniture stores.

Berkeley seemed divided into two individual parts long before the superhighway I-70 compounded the schism. There was lower Berkeley, south of the lake to West 38th Avenue, and there was Berkeley Hill, on the side and top of that long ridge that ran through the town. There was little contact between the two areas. The residents rode different streetcar lines to downtown, they attended different churches, and the children at-

The two Berkeley School buildings

Denver Public Schools

tended separate public schools. The school for lower Berkeley was the imposing Louisa M. Alcott Elementary School, at West 41st and Tennyson Street, built in 1892; the Berkeley Hill children went to Berkeley School at West 50th Avenue and Lowell Boulevard. This school, when first organized, met in a residence at

5101 Meade, later in a two room red brick building facing 51st, and then in a handsome school on the same grounds but facing Lowell, just north of 50th Avenue. Not until February, 1976 did the children meet in the same school, when Centennial School at West 47th and Raleigh Street was opened, combining the two districts

Great Western Post Card & Novelty Co.

A tent colony for tuberculars. This was the YMCA camp, which had an artesian well in the center.

and abandoning the two older buildings of Alcott and Berkeley. The night of March 25, 1976, Alcott School was destroyed by an arson-set fire, the day before it was to fall to the wrecker's ball. The fate of the Berkeley buildings at this writing is undecided.

The clear pure air attracted tuberculars to Berkeley as it did to Highlands, and there was a large tent colony at about 45th and Zenobia Street. These tents were permanent residences for the patients. The tents had wooden floors and wooden walls up about four feet on all sides, with canvas sides and tops, for fresh air was the only known cure, and here the many sick tuberculars lived day and night.

The town of Berkeley had a little trouble with its liquor restrictions. Their $1,000 license fee was not enough to keep some people from applying, but the town meeting had authority to turn down any applications. Some owners of the many vacant lots felt the liquor fee would help the tax situation, but the council was adamant. There was a strong chapter of the Women's Christian Temperance Union in Berkeley, and they served as watchdogs over the sale of liquor. On one occasion there was a rumor that a druggist was dispensing whiskey for other than medicinal purposes. Two determined members of the WCTU went to the drugstore and one ordered a dime's worth of quinine for a cold and then presented a bottle for a quarter's worth of whiskey. The druggist filled the bottle. If he had mixed the quinine and whiskey — an accepted remedy for colds — or if he had asked who was sick and needed the liquor, he would have been clear. But, since he had not, the ladies presented the evidence to the town magistrate and the druggist was fined $200.

There was a very popular family resort and dance hall on the south side of Berkeley Lake. Hearing rumors that people had seen kegs of beer delivered to the resort, these same two ladies, sincere and dedicated in their purpose, dressed in their long black skirts, white shirtwaists and plumed hats, braved this possible den of iniquity on a Sunday afternoon. It must have taken courage for either of them to order a glass of beer, but they did — and were served. They presented this evidence to the town marshal. One can't help wondering how they presented it. Was the marshal hiding behind a nearby bush and did the ladies run out to him with the full glasses? Surely they wouldn't have sipped it and had the marshal smell their breaths. Sadly, the newspaper account did not tell, but it did relish the story of the trial, when, it said, the prosecuting attorney was so drunk that he almost fell off the streetcar. The resort keeper was fined $50, which he appealed. Finally, his fine was suspended on the promise of good behavior and the assurance that no more sales of beer would be made by him from then on. In 1894 the city council changed Berkeley's liquor license fee to $3,000.

Denver had made various attempts to annex Berkeley, without success; but in 1902, when the city and county of Denver was created by the state legislature, Berkeley was included, without a vote of the people. At the time the town had a population of only 707 and was still largely rural. Most of its interesting growth came after it was part of Denver.

Berkeley Park was acquired piecemeal by the city from private owners, some as early as 1906. The city gradually improved it, especially under Mayor Speer's administration. Grass was planted, playgrounds put in, the lake dredged, dirt dumped on the swampy area at the east end of the lake. There was a rock garden and a memorial grove to the pioneers of the area, but these can no longer be identified. The Berkeley Family Resort and dance hall, of course, was discontinued, but a large pavilion and bathhouse was built at about the same location in 1913. The cottage style Smiley Branch Library was built in the park in 1918.

Swimming and ice skating were the seasonal attractions at Berkeley Park. A pier, later used only for fishing, extended into the lake, and large crowds swam (before the years when the city tested the water and declared it hygienically unsafe). In 1974 the parks department built a 25 meter outdoor swimming pool southwest of the lake. In the winters of those earlier years, a warming shelter was built at the edge of the lake (previous to the time the city began testing the ice thickness before permitting skating). Here skaters thawed out and skates were rented or sharpened. Many large crowds skated the old year out, the new year in, and dated, cracked the whip, raced, and did fancy figure skating any cold winter night. In 1913 there was also a ski jump in the park.

In 1910 the advent of airplanes excited Denver. During that summer a monoplane was built and tried out. It had a forced landing in Berkeley Lake, which drenched the flyers and plane, but also spawned an idea. They fitted it with pontoons and this first amphibian plane in Denver flew successfully for several months, sometimes from Berkeley, sometimes from Sloan's Lake.

In 1909 the city bought the top of Inspiration Point, the dramatic end of the long ridge that ran through Berkeley, overlooking the Clear Creek valley. The Point lay just across the county line of Sheridan from Berkeley Park. The city built a cement retaining wall around the top, put out markers to indicate various mountains that could be seen, and it became a popular place for daytime viewing of peaks and sunsets, as well as a favorite place for young couples seeking a quiet romantic spot in the evenings.

A private club, the Interlachen Country Club, in 1902 had established a rather primitive golf course on the slopes of Inspiration Point. This was a nine hole course with sand greens on ridges which projected from the Point like fingers. It was necessary to shoot across the gully to the hole on the next ridge. If the ball went into the gully, the player just considered it lost. These gulches had many round glacially formed small rocks covered with a white deposit, and if the ball was not lost among these rocks, it would disappear among the tufts of

Bob Bond

Smiley Public Library in Berkeley Park

buffalo grass, yucca, or prickly pear cactus, or into the gumbo mud, or down a rabbit or gopher hole. About 1911 the Interlachen officers entered into a contract with the city of Denver to develop another nine-hole course north of Berkeley Lake, with the city and the club sharing expenses of building and maintenance. At least one of these fairways was across a gravel pit. They now had an 18-hole course, which was open to the public except on Saturdays, Sundays, and holidays. Later the Shriners put in a nine-hole course on the north slope of the ridge where they had built a new mosque. By 1929 the Interlachen club had ceased to exist, and the city

175

A holiday swimming crowd at Berkeley Lake

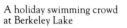

The whole mountain range could be seen from Inspiration Point

took over the eastern nine holes. The Shrine course was also added to the city's, all of it becoming the Willis Case golf course.

While Inspiration Point was still stark and rocky and unplanted with the present ponderosa pines, there was a simple red brick house at the top of a slope, visible for miles. It was the reputed, and apparently well-exposed, love nest established for a Denver and later nationally known actress, by a Denver man of affairs — business as well as personal — a politician, and companion of the so-called greats of the city. Many years later attractive and landscaped homes of all types were scattered about the slopes and top of the point.

The areas at the base of the Point were gradually annexed by Denver for residences, annexations being made in 1948, 1962, and 1969. The homes have almost enveloped the Camp Fire Girls' Camp Rollandet (named for an attorney, Jack Rollandet), a rustic camp located on ten acres on the north slope of the point. The area previously had been a dump, but about 1938 the Kiwanis Club and the girls worked to clean up, and with money provided by the Kiwanis, they moved in two surplus barracks buildings from Buckley Field, covered them with logs, built a rustic fireplace, drilled a 325 foot well, and had a delightful lodge and dormitory. It is still used as a day camp and for conferences, but is hardly the rural location it was originally.

Berkeley was so far away from the business center of Denver that it was necessarily a streetcar town. One line, for the Berkeley Dummy described in the chapter on Highlands and begun in 1888, met the cable cars at the barns at 30th and Zuni Street and traveled approximately the route the Berkeley bus does today. The West End Electric line, as mentioned before, met the cable cars at West Colfax and Utica Street and traveled north on Sheridan, past Manhattan Beach and Elitch Gardens to Berkeley Park. The West End Electric had its power house in Berkeley, north of West 38th Avenue between Utica and Tennyson Streets, across from Elitch Gardens. Car barns faced Tennyson. They later became the Leyden Coal Company. The dynamo house, at the corner of Utica and 38th, has become a familiar building in Berkeley. The 1890 Sanborn's Atlas shows it as housing three dynamos with offices at the east end of the building. Later, after the West End Electric had become

part of the Denver Tramway system, the building was leased by the National Guard, who put in a good hardwood floor. Known to everyone as "the Armory", the building was used for many things. Holy Family Catholic Church, newly organized in 1906, held a ten day fair in the Armory to raise money toward a church building. Wheat Ridge High School, with no gym of its own, used the Armory for basketball games. It was a roller skating rink, a dance hall, a fight ring, the front section was an orangeade stand, the east end was living quarters, and for the last twenty-five years the building has been a large garage.

Another streetcar line served Berkeley Hill. It was called the Rocky Mountain Lake line. At that then undeveloped park, the car turned on a Y, and with the motorman standing at the rear end, the car backed to West 50th and Stuart Street.

The Denver Tramway had coal mines at Leyden, about fifteen miles northwest of Denver, and daily coal trains traveled from the mines to the power house on the Platte River, using electric engines, and following the Berkeley streetcar lines. All wheels of all streetcars squealed as they went around corners, screaming on the steel rails, and a track swabber with his bucket of grease and black mop was a regular sight, but the coal trains squealed so loudly that anyone within several blocks of a turn in the track could count the screeches and know how many cars were in that particular train. The power house, at 1416 Platte Street in old North Denver, despite its industrial use, was a well proportioned red brick building with arched windows. It was built in 1901, is a designated landmark, and since 1969 has been the Forney Museum of antique transportation vehicles.

Berkeley was principally a town of hard-working home-owning individuals, with few wealthy or famous residents. By the time it was built, the Capitol Hill area east of downtown Denver was the socially accepted address, but for those who wanted the quiet and the fresh air of a moderate country suburb, it was ideal.

One famous person who grew up in Berkeley — in fact, grew to a very large size, was Don Wilson, announcer and sometimes straight man for radio and television comedian, Jack Benny. Don father's, Lincoln Wilson, owned the Alcott Pharmacy at 3973 Tennyson Street, and their home was at 3841 Wolff Street, a broad

The West End Electric dynamo house and cars at West 38th and Utica

brown brick luxuriant bungalow of the 1920's, whose horizontal lines and heavy porch pillars are in strong contrast to the Victorian houses about it.

One resident of Berkeley Hill was a man whose name is threaded profusely through the history of early Denver. He was Judge Hiram P. Bennet, who spent his last years in the home of his son at the top of the hill at 5084 Tennyson. Hiram P. Bennet was born in Maine in 1826 but grew up in Ohio and Missouri. He was a man of the frontier. He studied law while teaching school in Missouri, and then gradually worked his way west, practic-

ing law in Iowa and in Nebraska and serving on the Nebraska territorial legislature. When he arrived at the cluster of tents and log cabins known as Auraria, he showed his knowledge of the frontier, for he had brought with him equipment for a sawmill, and he and a partner immediately set up the mill about thirty miles southeast of town. There was always a demand for lumber in those rapidly growing towns at Cherry Creek and the Platte, and the sawmills were constantly busy. Mr. Bennet practiced law in Denver and was the prosecuting attorney in the Peoples' Court, which administered speedy

Bob Bond

The home of Don Wilson's parents on Wolff Street

justice to the outlaws and desperadoes who harassed the little towns. Later he served two terms as the territorial delegate to Congress, where, although he had no vote, he spoke so forcefully and eloquently that he saved Colorado's budding mining industry, and also assured a mint's being located in Denver. In addition, he was appointed Denver Postmaster from 1869 to 1874 and was a senator in the first Colorado General Assembly.

Judge Bennet was a man of great intelligence, New England shrewdness, and a quiet sense of humor. He was one of the few champions at that time of the American Indian and was an escort of Chief Ouray of the Utes to

179

The modest Bennet residence

Washington to plead for the Indians' cause. He first became acquainted with Chief Ouray when he, with Richard Sopris (later a Denver mayor and the man for whom Mount Sopris is named) and Isaac Cooper explored the Roaring Fork Valley and the Western Slope. Bennet was instrumental in having the town which became Glenwood Springs surveyed, and he and Cooper, both from Glenwood, Iowa, named the new town for their home city. There is still a Bennet Avenue in Glenwood Springs, and there was a Cooper Avenue, which has been renamed Grand.

During the early years in Denver, Judge Bennet was disturbed by the very vocal southern sympathizers just before the outbreak of the Civil War. He knew that there were more, but silent, Union sympathizers, who needed a leader to rally them. On his own, he went to the mountains and brought down a thirty foot tree to be used as a flagpole. He traded a real estate lot he owned in Golden for a large flag, and on Washington's birthday, 1861, he rallied enthusiastic Union supporters about the flag which he planted in his front yard, on Ninth Street, between Lawrence and Curtis, Auraria.

He made an impassioned speech and provided about five gallons of "other stimulation" to bring out the latent patriotism. By the time the Civil War was declared, Colorado was strongly on the side of the Union Forces.

Judge Hiram Bennet after 1904 lived with his son at 5084 Tennyson, where he died when 83 years old, in 1909. When Jerome Smiley wrote his *History of Denver* in 1901, he said: "In the history of our city and state, especially in that part of it covering the pioneer era, the student will encounter few more interesting figures, few personalities of greater influence and usefulness in the community or that filled a larger place in the affairs and esteem of the people, than that of Hiram P. Bennet."

Judge Bennet and his wife had five children, one of whom was Robert Ames Bennet. Robert was a frail child, probably tubercular, and his education was partially furnished at home. When he was seven years old, the family moved temporarily to Deadwood, South Dakota, still very much the center of Sioux Country at that time. He did study and practice law, but could never develop much interest in it. Through his father's concern for the Indians, Robert's challenge lay in working with the natives. He spent a year as a clerk at Fort Belknap Reservation in Montana, a Blackfoot reservation. In his spare time he laid the framework for his later success as a writer of novelettes and historical novels. He wrote over fifty books, most of them translated into four or five European languages. In Europe they were even more popular than in this country. He was a close associate of many other Denver authors and one of the most successful of them.

Robert Ames Bennet outlived his childhood frailties, was an outdoorsman, and lived to be 84 years old, many of his years in the Berkeley Hill home. He and his wife had one son, Harold H., a successful structural engineer, who married and lived next door.

The eastern stretches of Berkeley Hill were slow in developing. Around 1910 there were only three houses between Regis College, at 50th and Lowell, and the Henry Weirich celery farm at the east end of Rocky Mountain Lake at West 48th and Federal.

The Weirich property was homesteaded by Harvey Bird, and bought by the Weirich family in January, 1900. The countryside was strictly rural in all directions. Federal Boulevard was a little dusty road, edged with a tangle of raspberry and blackberry bushes. Weirich, who had been in farming in the midwest, specialized in raising celery, developed a new strain, and was known as the celery king. Raising celery meant hard work, not only for the father, but for the two sons and two daughters, but, like country children everywhere, they found time for the pleasure of simple picnic lunches under the trees while they picked currants and gooseberries at a neighbor's farm, or learned the songs of the yellow headed blackbirds in the cattails along the lake. The Weirichs had one of the many greenhouses which existed all over Northwest Denver. While today most of these greenhouses specialize in Colorado carnations, the earlier ones raised necessities such as tomatoes and lettuce.

At the south side of Rocky Mountain Lake, in those early 1900's, there was a private park, owned by a Mrs. Taylor. She operated a dance pavilion on the shore, rowboats and a steamer on the lake. On a map of 1885 a "Belleview House" is shown on the north shore of the lake, but nothing further can be found about it. The south part of Rocky Mountain Park was developed under Mayor Speer, starting about 1910. It did not seem to be one of the favored parks of the system, and only recently has it been fully developed. Meantime, the superhighway I-70 has been cut along the north side of the lake.

Besides the trees in the two parks, the Berkeley area boasted many beautiful shade trees, orchards, and gardens. S. R. DeBoer, famous landscape gardener and city planner who lived in Northwest Denver, actually in Grand View, around 1914, was always interested in the area. He had hoped for a diagonal tree-lined boulevard, an extension of Speer Boulevard, to run to Berkeley Park, but this did not materialize. In 1915 he had American elms planted on both sides of Federal Boulevard from West Colfax to West 46th Avenue, partly at the instigation of George Olinger, president of the Olinger Mortuaries, and a civic minded person. (One of George Olinger's activities was to start the Highlander Boys organization, the name originating from the part of North Denver where the family business started.)

By the time the trees were planted along the sides of Federal, the center row of cottonwoods, started back in 1875 had been removed. In the 1950's, when Federal

The Rocky Mountains overlook their namesake lake

was widened, the elms in the side parkings, which De-Boer had cherished, were cut down. In S. R. DeBoer's story printed in the December, 1972, issue of the *Green Thumb*, published by the Denver Botanic Gardens, he said: "The story of the trees on Federal Boulevard I wish I could erase from my memory. I am not referring to planting the trees in the Speer years. I am referring to what happened 40 years afterward. The trees were fully grown but they had not been watered for several years. The traffic engineer wanted to widen the street and ordered the trees removed. I was on other work. The park engineer who had neglected the trees had them cut down. It was wholesale slaughter, and I am still ashamed that Denver could have an experience like this. The sad fact is that the street could have been widened without touching the trees."

Previous to that, though no one seems to know when, someone had planted a handsome row of cottonwoods down the center of what became West 44th Avenue, from Lowell west to Stuart or Tennyson. Perhaps it was a windbreak for some early farm. People called the street "Lovers' Lane." But it became the scene of a tragedy January 2, 1923, when Father Farrell, priest at Holy Family Church, driving home after conducting a wedding in South Denver, skidded into one of these trees and was killed. During the great depression, in 1933, these 44th Avenue trees fell victims to "self-help" work, providing firewood for needy families. Members of the House of David, a religious sect in Denver, worked on contract with the city to fell the trees. Incidentally, these same people had an excellent baseball team, and with their patriarchial beards flying in the wind, would make running the bases a spectacular sight.

Home gardens, both flower and vegetable, were important to the people in Berkeley. *Municipal Facts,* publication of the city of Denver, in 1913 reported that a Mrs. S. B. Walker, at 3857 Xavier, had over 200 varieties of Colorado wild flowers in her garden. The wild flowers seem to be gone now, but the little brown house has magnificent evergreen trees in the yard, no doubt also started by Mrs. Walker. Somewhere in Berkeley lived a little man from India who was an herb doctor. Every inch of his yard was planted with exotically fragrant plants and shrubs. He concocted medicines from knowledge he had brought from India, and before present days of strict control of medications, he periodically drove about the city in his horse and buggy delivering potions, and reports of his cures were frequent.

Small, neat, white frame houses, interspersed with Victorian two-stories, and a few broad-verandahed brick bungalows — this is lower Berkeley today. It seems not so much a part of a big city as a quiet self-respecting midwestern town. Paint is fresh and clean, flower boxes and gardens smile with color, lawns are trimmed. Lower Berkeley, as well as Berkeley Hill, has pockets of homes of the affluent, either past or present. Wherever there was a view of the mountains, there lovely homes were

Denver Public Library, Western History Department
Looking east along 44th Avenue

built. In the 1930's and 40's some large attractive houses were built near the Willis Case Golf Course, or on the ridge overlooking Clear Creek Valley. Marching along beside them are neat little cottages of individualistic design of each period of architecture since the 1880's, including an occasional tall Victorian, which may have been some of those designed by William Lang.

The unincorporated areas

Lying between Berkeley and Argo was farmland, and while there were real estate developments in some of the areas, none was ever incorporated. In 1893, the city of Denver, undoubtedly seeing themselves more and more hemmed in by small separate towns, annexed this large area, but while it was now part of the city, it was slow to develop.

Lovely homes were built wherever there was a view

Tucked into the southeast corner of the zigzagging east and south boundaries of lower Berkeley, lay Argyle Park, whose Scotch named streets of Lorne, Dumbarton, Inverness, Forth, Tweed, Tay, Clyde, and Dee indicate that John Brisben Walker and Dr. William A. Bell had some influence in this section. Argyle Park was established about 1889 or 1890. It was a place of scattered houses, being fairly close to two streetcar lines, but more than that it was a garden spot of cherry and apple orchards, of flower growers who raised riotous dahlias, cosmos, snapdragons, cannas, zinnias, and roses for sale. It was a site for shade trees, and the *Colorado Exchange*

Journal of October, 1889, said, "Ample streets and broad avenues are lined with from four to six rows of large trees, the growth of twenty years. The location is beautiful and the view of mountain scenery and suburban improvements unsurpassed. It is especially desirable for families with children, when the need for pure air and abundant shade is most keenly felt. A resident, W. E. Pabor, so famous as the possessor of true poetic fire, has written of this sylvan suburb:

"The shadows play in Argyle Park
  In slanting lines of gold and green;
The matin song of meadow lark
  Floats softly through the summer scene.

"The bees in the alfalfa rows
  Are busy gaining stores of sweets;
And cool the air of morning blows
  Between the tree-embowered streets.

"He who would all the comforts know
  Of country charm in city bounds
To beauteous Argyle Park should go
  And find it in its shaded grounds."

It is probably presumptuous to add anything to this burst of poetic fire. W. E. Pabor, who lived at the northwest corner of West 38th and Perry Streets, where a garage now stands, was editor and general manager of the periodical, *Colorado Farm and Fruit Growers.*

In the very southwest corner of Argyle Park, at West 38th and Tennyson, catty-corner from the main gate of Elitch's, was a semi-pro baseball field. Everyone during the turn of the century was crazy about baseball. Businesses sponsored teams and furnished uniforms, balls, bats, and masks. The crude bleachers were full of loudly cheering rooters every Sunday afternoon, the hat was passed for a donation to the players, and soda pop was hawked.

The subdivision of Argyle Park at first extended only from Tennyson to Perry Street, and from West 38th to West 44th. Later an addition broadened it to Lowell on the east, which went as far north as 41st Avenue. North of 41st, between Perry and Lowell, lay the grounds of St. Vincent's Orphanage, conducted by the Sisters of Char-

ity of Leavenworth. The building is still there, a large red brick affair, now used as a residential treatment center for boys and girls with emotional problems.

One striking home of Argyle Park is at the corner of West 38th and Raleigh Street. It was built in Georgian Colonial style by Dr. Charles J. Lowen, about 1915, and later was the home of the John Mulvihills and the Arnold Gurtlers, owners of Elitch Gardens. The grounds of this home have been meticulously kept, and the present owners continue to maintain a lovely home.

Across Raleigh Street is the Ladies Relief Society, more familiarly known as the Old Ladies' Home. The Society was organized in 1875 to give aid to women and children of Denver, and this building in 1898 replaced an earlier one at East Eighth Avenue and Logan. The suburb of Argyle Park made a beautiful setting for such a home, which has extremely large trees about its broad lawn.

East of Argyle Park, from Lowell to Federal, and from West 38th to West 41st, was a section known as Boulevard Place, with many individual owners. No one real estate promoter handled this part, and it was developed in bits and pieces. One large tract, between Irving and King, West 40th to 41st, was the site selected for the second junior high school in the city. Skinner, built in 1922, was named for Miss Elizabeth Skinner, a long-time and loved teacher whose home had always been in Highlands.

North of Boulevard Place was Harkness Heights, publicized as the Capitol Hill of North Denver. Bounded by 41st to 44th and Lowell to Federal, it was probably named for Charles Harkness, an early owner, who is listed in the city directory of 1874 as being a candle manufacturer. Harkness Heights was developed by John McDonough, the young Englishman who was sent to Denver by the Kansas City syndicate which bought the Berkeley Farm from John Brisben Walker. John McDonough became one of the leading businessmen of Denver, active in commerce, banking, mining, real estate, and in civic organizations. He was president of the Denver Chamber of Commerce, the Real Estate Exchange, and the Advertising Men's Club. When the Panic of 1893 stopped business in Denver, McDonough went to Creede where he was president of a bank. He returned about 1902 and promoted Harkness Heights. It

The charming Mulvihill-Gurtler home in Argyle Park

never became a Capitol Hill, a place of mansions, but many substantial upper middle-class houses were built. Most of them are of light colored brick with broad verandahs and of squarish construction, still a nice middle-class neighborhood. Many of the original home-owners were executives of large establishments, others developed their own businesses. The days of the fabulous empire builders were gone, but these were the people who helped change ebullient Denver into a solid city.

John McDonough in 1908 built his own spacious home two blocks from Harkness Heights, at the corner of West 46th and Perry Street. It is a broad white two

Bob Bond

Skinner Junior High was the second junior high in Denver

story house with french windows, red tile roof, and extensive grounds. Four years later McDonough was driving his car home for lunch one summer day in 1912 when, while crossing the 14th Street (Speer) viaduct, he had a heart attack and died immediately. Mrs. McDonough carried on his business for several years.

John Malm, a civic leader and Boy Scout executive, lived in the former McDonough home until his death in 1926. The house later was occupied by an order of nuns, then again reverted to a private residence.

For conservative Northwest Denver to boast a community theater, which has been in existence over fifty

John McDonough lived in his spacious home only four years before his death

years, seems a little startling. It sprang, however, from conservative and practical beginnings. George Swartz had wanted to be an actor from the time he was a boy in his home in Pennsylvania. The idea was shocking to his parents, so he became a teacher. Tuberculosis brought him to Colorado, to a little house at 3440 Clay Street,

in the early 1900's. He developed a unique method of improving and healing his lungs by breathing large quantities of fresh air. For this he turned to declamation. He had always loved Shakespearean plays, so he started memorizing them, striding about the house, proclaiming verbatim in a loud voice all the lines of eight of Shake-

The Gaslight Theater began as the Bungalow Theater

speare's dramas. This had two results — his tuberculosis was arrested; and neighbors and friends began coming to the house to listen and applaud. His wife made costumes to fit each of his characters, and she and their daughters served grape juice and homemade cookies.

In 1911 Swartz built a new home at 4201 Hooker Street in Harkness Heights. It was built in the style of the day, of light brick with a broad verandah, but there is a difference. In the basement Swartz constructed as nearly perfect a little theater as he could, which he called the Bungalow Theater. The house and the theater are still there (now called the Gaslight Theater). It's an intimate place, seating only a hundred people, the stage nine feet high and fifteen feet deep, with an 18-foot proscenium opening. Swartz produced and directed over eight hundred plays here in a period of twenty years, drilling the amateur casts to absolute perfection. The Bungalow Theater is one of the few theaters in the world to have presented everything Shakespeare wrote. Swartz' wife and daughters helped out with costumes, prompting, painting sets. The atmosphere was informal. Between acts the Swartzes served the usual grape juice and homemade cookies in their living quarters upstairs. The Bungalow Theater was not for profit, not at admission prices of five cents, which over the years gradually grew to twenty cents, but Swartz loved it, and so did Northwest Denver, and Swartz gave drama lessons to help with finances.

George Swartz died of a heart attack in 1937. But the theater lived on. In the early 1940's Paul Willett, who had directed the Lowry Field Players at that army air force base in Denver, opened a theatrical training school. With the very valuable help of friends, Dr. and Mrs. Robert A. Bradley, of Englewood, the Bungalow Theater was restored and renamed Actors Studio 29, which Willett directed from 1955 to 1957. Another group took over the theater for a few years, then Paul Willett returned in 1964, serving as producer, director, set designer, sometimes actor, as well as a teacher and coach. He has presented nearly fifty plays at the refurbished basement theater, now called the Gaslight, in this quiet middle class neighborhood. Some of the plays have been controversial, some experimental, some psychological. Many have been "firsts" for Denver. There have been comedies, tragedies, and mysteries. The plays run a minimum of two months and some much longer. The theater, with a semi-pro and professional cast, is internationally known, and Willett receives scripts from all over the world. The audiences which come from every part of the Denver area are very loyal and they love the informality of before acts in the garden, the between acts traditional refreshments upstairs, and the art exhibits which hang on the walls of Willett's parlor and library.

North of Harkness Heights, from 44th to 46th Avenues, from Federal to Lowell Boulevard, lies Grand View, another subdivision which is, in certain blocks,

Grand View corner post

190

more prestigious than Harkness Heights, for some very fine homes were built along the borders of Rocky Mountain Park in the 1930's and 40's. The subdivision itself was developed in the 1910's and 20's by Mauritz E. Carlson, a contractor, and on each street corner of the section is a brick post, about five feet tall, with the words, "Grand View," inscribed on terra cotta. The name of the area may have had much humbler beginnings; Smiley's *History of Denver* says: "The Board of Directors [of School District No. 17] also added that year [1883] to the school equipment an ugly little frame structure near Rocky Mountain Lake on a plot of one and one-quarter acres of land which they bought cheap. This house was grandiloquently named the 'Grand View School'." Nevertheless, there was a grand view of the Rocky Mountains across this watering hole-turned irrigation reservoir-turned city lake, a view that sadly now is interrupted by the superhighway I-70.

Scattered about Grand View, before the real estate development got under way, were small self-sustaining homes, usually simple brick, surrounded by a patch of lawn, flower gardens, a kitchen garden of vegetables, a chicken house and yard, possibly a small barn, probably a privy in the backyard, and certainly the inevitable clothesline. Life in these homes, just as in every other part of Denver at the same time, had a security and constancy about it. They produced their own vegetables and fruits for the mammoth — but satisfying — job in the fall of canning, drying, and preserving, they raised their own eggs and the chickens for the usual Sunday dinner, made and remade their own clothes. The fathers were skilled laborers, or held clerical, teaching, or minor executive jobs, some of the women were teachers, some were music teachers, or dressmakers. There were worries about mortgage payments, illnesses, death — especially from tuberculosis; but in all it was a secure semi-rural community that the residents loved.

Today Harkness Heights and Grand View seem to be much alike, with some older homes of the Victorian era — many remodeled, the sturdy square red brick houses of the turn of the century, the later roomy friendly bungalows, interspersed with a few elegant residences.

East of Federal to Zuni, from 44th to 48th, was the large farm of Lewis K. Perrin. South of this to 38th was Perrin's Addition, which we may also assume was part of the Perrin farm. Perrin was one of Colorado's earliest successful farmers. He had come to the Arvada-Wheat Ridge area first, then moved to Northwest Denver in 1875. He was one of the first farmers to plant sugar beets, and won many agricultural prizes in the state. Perrin built a beautiful large Italianate home on a hill, of which the present address would be 4375 Clay Street. The house had a delicate iron fence around the widow's walk on a low tower and was landscaped with pines and maples. There was an orchard, a grape arbor, and the indispensable kitchen garden. The family had a deep, 850 feet, artesian well on the property, and water was piped to neighbors as far away as 41st and Alcott. The Perrin place was an ideal suburban home of the 1880's and 90's.

Lewis Perrin planted a windbreak of cottonwoods along 44th Avenue, and legend tells of one of these which became a "robber tree." The trees were large, traffic was scanty. But, travelers who had the appearance of affluence approached the intersection of the country roads, now known as Federal and West 44th, with caution. More than once, in broad daylight, a highwayman would suddenly appear before the horse and rider, or buggy and driver, quickly take all valuables, and disappear. Where had he come from? Where did he go? How could he tell some passersby had money while laborers or farmers went unmolested? At last someone realized that the robber was hiding in the branches of one of the big cottonwoods, where he could watch the roads in all directions and pick the wealthier-appearing travelers, then he would jump down abruptly to accost his victim, and disappear just as quickly, back into the foliage. The tree was a handsome one and stood until streets were widened in 1927, but the robber's career was cut down quickly.

Lewis Perrin died in 1897, but before then the big farm was cut up into lots and acreages, and plots which were planted to strawberries, raspberries, asparagus, celery. Many of the large evergreens about the home were used as Denver's annual Civic Center Christmas trees. The house was later sold to the Strang family, who had several children, four boys and a girl, of whom all the boys went to Princeton and became successful professional and businessmen. In 1958 the lovely old house was razed, and the site used for a filling station.

Columbian School built in 1892

The growth of the neighborhoods on both sides of Federal (the Boulevard) is apparent by the addition of another elementary school, Columbian, at West 40th and Federal, which was built in 1892. It is now slated for replacement.

Old maps show other small developments, north of the early original North Denver. A small three-block square section, just north of 38th to 41st and from Pecos to Tejon (then called Clear Creek Avenue to Goss Avenue) was named Sunnyside, a name which the present Planning Commission of the City of Denver has selected to indicate the large section from West 38th to I-70, and from I-25 to Federal Boulevard.

Another development, platted in blocks, was called

Denver Public Schools

Beach Court School built in 1950

North Highlands (no relation to the early elite town of Highlands). Its boundaries were Zuni on the west to Pecos on the east, 44th on the south (then called Gaston Avenue) to 48th (then North Boulevard). The east-west streets sound like a wild life preserve: Antelope, Bison, Coyote, Deer, and Elk, but it again was an area of small scattered Victorian houses, now interspersed with newer small homes.

West 48th Avenue seemed to be the edge of the world; some real estate maps did not show beyond it at all. However, between 48th and 52nd (the county line after 1902) there were truck farms and small homes. Another elementary school, Beach Court, was started in two cottages in this area in 1921, and a new building at 50th and Beach Court, was built in 1950.

A world war came and things were never the same

Remington Elementary School

again in Denver, nor anywhere, and certainly not in the quiet little stretch of country to the city limits of Denver, a place where there had been cottonwood groves for picnics, and self-sufficient little farms, and where sand lilies, johnny-jump-ups, prickly pear cactus, golden banner, loco, chiming bells, and wild pink roses made the air fragrant until the hot summer sun took over and replaced the dainty spring flowers with sunflowers and Russian thistles.

World War II brought a greater influx of people to the Denver area than it had seen since the first gold rush days. The areas between West 48th and West 52nd Avenues, east of Zuni, had started to grow in the 1930's. But it was during the war years and immediately after when Chaffee Park, north of 48th, had most of its growth. Chaffee Park was an unusual phenomenon for Northwest Denver. Previously most houses had been built as needed and to the owner's taste. Now Chaffee Park became a new section of homogenous frame houses, of repetitive designs, altered by being placed on curving streets — the first curving streets Northwest Denver had had since 1875. Military families arrived, most of them with babies, who, in a few years, created the need for a new school, and Remington Elementary, at Pecos and West 47th Avenue, was built in 1955. This was the last new (not replacement) elementary school built in the northwest sector.

Thankfully, the last few years have seen a renewed interest in older homes. Many young people have warmed to the grace and solid construction of all the different sections of Northwest Denver's older homes, a treasure trove of Victorian and turn-of-the-century houses. People, young and old, with growing families or established careers, industrious ways and a personal feeling for our heritage can be found living in more and more of the well-loved homes north and west of the confluence of Cherry Creek and the South Platte River, as far as the city limits reach.

Conclusion

It has been a bad habit of mine not to read the preface until I've read the contents of a book. Then, if I like what I read, I go back to the preface. Since few people are unique in their habits, I'm sure others share this one with me. For us contrary individuals, I've named my preface "Conclusion" and have placed it at the end, hoping you have enjoyed reading the story of Northwest Denver enough to want to know a bit about the writing of the book — which is, really, the purpose of a preface.

I have long been interested in the history of the northwest sector of the city, where I have lived since I was about ten years old, when I would fantasize about the intriguing houses I passed on my way to Edison School. I have probably been as proud as any of the people mentioned in the book, and have suffered when the media called us by the wrong geographic designation, or when people have said, "You live in *North* Denver?" with an inflection which, to my supersensitive pride, seemed to imply "slums," or "off the edge." It has been amazing to me that many families who live in other sections of Denver have never crossed a viaduct to see this part of the city, unless it was to attend Elitch Gardens, which is a beautiful part but not all of Northwest Denver.

It was probably with all this in mind that, after writing magazine articles on many subjects for years, I wrote "Highlands, Denver's Rival Utopia," which was published in *Empire Magazine* March 31, 1968. I then had other writing I planned to do. But that was not to be the end of my story of Highlands. I was asked, first, by the North Denver Woman's Club, and then by the Denver Public Library, to give talks on the subject. My husband and I scurried around to take color slides; more calls came, and to date we have shown the slides and told the story of Highlands and the other parts of Northwest Denver sixty-one times, not only in this particular section of the city, but over the metropolitan area.

My information has grown and grown, for at almost every lecture someone in the audience added to the story. I learned to verify and authenticate everything I was told, for memories can be tricky on dates and details. There have been some fascinating bits I have left out, because they were not the kind of stories that could be verified or could not be included as a rumor or legend.

As I gave the lectures, it was never my intention to write a book. But more and more people asked the delicately morbid question, "What's going to happen to all this information when you're not around?"; so I finally concluded it should be written, not so much for posterity as for the people of the present, that they might learn of a unique piece of Denver's geography and history which has never been included in any other book.

I labeled this chapter "Conclusion," but there really can be no final statement in the story of an area which is still alive and viable. However, I have come to some conclusions. The first is obvious: that Northwest Denver

is a rare treasury of Victorian and turn-of-the-century houses, still well loved and well kept. Of course, there are those that are ramshackle, poorly maintained, or poorly built in the first place, and better torn down. Not all are historical; in fact, some are quite new. On the few vacant lots left, some very attractive homes of the 1970's have been built, for the same reasons for which people built their homes in the 80's, 90's, and through the 1950's — the air, the water, the view, the friendly people. I wish I could have written of more houses and families, there are such a number of interesting ones. I wish I could have covered all the institutions, but each one has a long story of its own, and I can only hope that these bodies have written the stories while there are those here who know the beginnings and the struggles.

Another conclusion I have drawn is that Denver was built much more on tuberculosis and the area's great asset of pure air than it was on the assets of precious metals. Let's hope that the same vigor can be exhibited in preserving that air as was shown in hunting and mining the gold and silver.

I have not attempted to write of sociological or other urban problems. They certainly do exist in Northwest Denver and deserve our serious and immediate attention. The only problem I have tried to present is the one of preservation of the traditions, the homes, trees, gardens, views, beauty and pride that made up Northwest Denver.

Acknowledgements

My first interest in Northwest Denver was aroused by my mother, Louise Barrows Lowe, who lived briefly in Highlands as a young girl, about 1891. Her encouragement was never failing, and her last words to me, before she passed away two years ago, were "How is the book coming?" Her help has been augmented by many people. One of the first was Pearl Queree, who herself had started such a history and tragically had her materials accidentally destroyed. Miss Queree died a few months before this book was finished, and I feel deep regret that I cannot tell her now how much she helped. There are others, however, to whom I have always been able to turn with numerous questions or for verification, and to three especially, Anne Mackay, Jeannette Bennetts, and Walter Lehrer, I do say a huge "Thank you!"

But where can I stop? So many others have spent hours with me, narrating, reminiscing, clarifying, encouraging, allowing pictures, that the only fair thing I can do is to list them alphabetically, for each one's help has been indispensable. Sometimes in the confusion following a lecture, someone has given me a precious bit of information that was like a missing piece in a jigsaw puzzle, but I did not get his or her name. I may also have accidentally omitted someone else. To these who must be anonymous, thanks! Others to whom I am indebted are many: William Alexander, Jack and Lois Anthony, Louisa Ward Arps, Bill Barker, Vivienne Barrett, Harry Barrows*, Harold Bennet* and Edith Bennet, Homer Berger, Helen Black, Patricia Black, Eddie Bohn, Francis Bosco, the Reverend Roy A. Carlson, Walden Carlson*, Edward Carr of the City of Denver Design Engineering, Rudy Castro of the City Planning Commission, Alice Coleman, Brian Congleton, Aleyne Coppers, Corinne Cottrell, Loma and Irving Creighton, Edith Dunwoody, Laura Eckstrom, William Ellis*, Dr. J. R. Feucht, Lorraine Finnicum, Doris Folkers, Frances Fuller, Joanne and Dennis Gallagher, Sister Getulia, O.F.F., William C. Gibson, Agnes Smedley Gieseke, Allene Gorman, Bob Green of Mother of Guadalupe Church, Clara Groff, John Gurtler, Sr., Bill Handley, Maude and Clifford Hauenstein, Opal Hold, Greg Hubbard, Clinton Jones*, William C. Jones, Mrs. Joseph Jonusis, Evelyn Jurcheck, Anna Kane, Mary Lou Keating, Grace Kenehan, Herbert Kennison, Roy Kent*, Penny Kenyon, Myron Lambert, Louise Lantzy, Dr. John Litvak, the Reverend H. A. Lycett, George McCormack*, Rudolph Maier, Frank Mancini, Pasquale Marranzino, Olga Marshall, Avesta Mauzey, Edith Merkl, Maurine Moody, Fred E. Neef, Margaret Noyes*, Mrs. E. F. Nussbaum, Ray E. Olson, Anthony Padilla, Hjalmer Persman, Lulita Pritchett, Hannchen Rahne, Dorothy Rankin, Velma Hoyt Reeve, Thomas A. Richardson, Charles W. Rische, Ruth Voorhees Robinson, Edna Rogers, Ann and Ray Romanski, Margaret and Orville Rowland, Barbara and David Sheldon, the Reverend Paul Small, Ruby Stocking, Charles Swanson, Kathy Tanko, Ida Uchill, Gwendolyn Olinger VanDerbur, the Reverend Gabriel M. Weber, Ruth Wheeler, David Wicks of the Denver Landmark Preservation Commission, Virginia Wiebenson, Paul Willett, Merinel Williams of Georgetown Historical Society, Merrill Wilson, Grace Lobach Woodbury.

Nearly at the end of the alphabet comes the Wiberg (pronounced, please, as Weberg) family: my husband, my sons, and their wives. There just isn't any way I can thank them sufficiently for the patience, the moral and material support, the help they have given in taking pictures, driving every street of Northwest Denver, taking innumerable phone calls, reading or listening to and discussing manuscript, correcting proof, and putting up with bursts of frustration, discouragement, panic, or just plain bad temperament.

Of course, I want to add the complete staff of the Western History Department of the Denver Public Library as recipients of heartfelt thanks. I have been checking, rechecking, and dredging up little nuggets of facts at the Western History Department for so long that many staff changes have been made. But to all — retired, moved, or present members of the staff, I want to say that without your friendly and consistently helpful attitude, this book would not have been written.

The Denver Public Schools, Department of Press and Media Relations, have also been most generous with pictures and information, which is greatly appreciated.

My photographers, Errol Salter, Hallie Bond, and Bob Bond, and graphic designer, Elizabeth Hickler, deserve more than a mention of their names on the copyright page. They have my deepest appreciation for all they have done, quite often far beyond the requirements of their duties.

*Now deceased

Past and Present Street Names

You will find, in some instances, several names given for the same street, simply because the various developers showed remarkable independence and ingenuity in the naming of their streets. It is not practical to list them according to subdivisions, but I believe they can be found on the map at the front of the book.

The Original North Denver

In 1904 the north-south streets west of Broadway were given the present Indian names, arranged aphabetically, starting with Acoma. North Denver streets, because of the river, industries, undeveloped land, and railroad tracts (and now Highway I-70), start with Inca:

North-south:

Present name	Former name or names
Inca	Merrill
Jason	Converse
Kalamath	Somands
Lipan	Justine
Mariposa	Clifton
Navajo	Palmer
Osage	Bell
Pecos	Clear Creek
Quivas, Raritan	Witter, Vine, Lee
Shoshone	Arlington
Tejon	Goss
Umatilla	Mary, Forest
Vallejo	Bert, Burt, Wall
Wyandot	Gray, Vincent
Zuni	Gallup

The diagonal streets as originally laid out by General Larimer were considered extensions of the streets in Auraria, with the same names. They were renamed in 1881, with the names they bear today — from the river north: Water, Platte, Central, Boulder, Erie, Kensing Court.

In North Denver blocks were numbered from Gallup east; i.e., Gallup to Gray 00 block; Gray to Bert 100; Bert to Mary 200, etc.

East-west:

Present name	Former name or names
West 26th Ave.	Pierce
West 27th Ave.	Francis
West 28th Ave.	John
West 29th Ave.	Ashland
West 30th Ave.	Fay
West 31st Ave.	Bigler
West 32nd Ave.	Fairview
West 33rd Ave.	Wanless
West 34th Ave.	Kent
West 35th Ave.	Scott
West 36th Ave.	Murdock
West 37th Ave.	Euclid, Backus

West 38th Ave.	Prospect
West 39th Ave.	Beecher
West 40th Ave.	Greeley
West 41st Ave.	Dakota, Humphrey
West 42nd Ave.	Colorado
West 43rd Ave.	Wyoming
West 44th Ave.	Curtis, Gaston, Dee
West 45th Ave.	Antelope, Almina
West 46th Ave.	Bison
West 47th Ave.	Coyote, Augusta
West 48th Ave.	Deer, Marguret
West 49th Ave.	Elk
West 50th Ave.	North Blvd.

Streets of Highlands

The north-south streets, following Denver City Ordinance #19, dated February 18, 1904, were named alphabetically, with names of prominent people. Previously streets had carried many different names, and in various subdivisions streets did not meet squarely those in the next development. For that reason, there may be some divergencies.

North-south:

Present name	Former name or names
Zuni	Gallup (100 block)
Alcott	2nd, Stewart (200 block)
Bryant	3rd, Tracy
Clay	4th, Gibson
Decatur	5th, Taylor
Eliot	6th, Morgan
—	Longfellow
Federal	Boulevard, Boulevard F
Grove	7th, Clark, Black, Oak
Hazel Court	8th, Indiana
Hooker	9th, Florence, Ash
Irving	10th, Ann, Walnut
Julian	11th, May, Willow
King	12th, Hunley, Cedar
Lowell	13th, Williams, Lake, Berkeley, Spring, Homer, Spruce
Meade	14th, Winfield, Janet, Laurel
Newton	15th, Wolff, Willow
Osceola	16th, Colorado, Rose
Perry	17th, Gray, McCormic, Sterling, Prairie
Quitman	18th, Manning, Inverness
Raleigh	19th, Anderson, Lorne
Stuart	20th, Cooper, Dumbarton
Tennyson	21st, Delaware, Greenwood, Maple, Canby, Lake, Berkeley
Utica	22nd, Earl, Andes
Vrain	23rd, Lafayette, Lake, Oak, Sierra Nevada
Wolff or Winona Ct.	24th, Park, Lane, Elaine, Mohawk, Rose
Xavier	25th, Fairbury
Yates	26th, Lake
Zenobia	Susquehanna

East-west streets also varied in different subdivisions. These are the most common names.

East-west:

Present name	Former name or names
W. Colfax Avenue	Colfax Avenue, South Golden Road
Conejos Pl.	Conejos Avenue (100 block)
—	Center
W. 16th Avenue	Cheltenham (200 block)
W. Annie Pl.	Annie
W. 17th Avenue	Ellsworth, Grand View
W. 18th Avenue	Saguache
W. 19th Avenue	Chicago
W. 20th Avenue	Carbon
W. 21st Avenue	Jasper
W. 22nd Avenue	Pearl
W. 23rd Avenue	Agate
W. 24th Avenue	Ruby, Topaz
W. Byron Pl.	W. Byron, Pearce
W. 25th Avenue	Emerald, Granite
W. 26th Avenue	Highland
W. 27th Avenue	Diamond
W. 28th Avenue	Garnet, Pearl
W. 29th Avenue	Ashland
W. Hayward Place	Hayward, Minion
W. 30th Avenue	Dawson, Summit, Elgin, Cactus
W. 31st Avenue	Arkins, Brevier, Gerspeach
W. 32nd Avenue	Fairview, Blaine
W. Moncrieff Pl.	Moncrieff, Niagara, Worth
W. 33rd Avenue	Clinton, Wanless
W. 34th Avenue	Hawthorn, Brynn Mawr, Inverness Wayne, Kent
W. 35th Avenue	Monticello, Cumberland
W. 36th Avenue	Scott
W. 37th Avenue	Valley, Backus, Euclid, Van Buren
W. Clyde Place	Clyde Vale
W. 38th Avenue	Prospect

Streets Names in Berkeley, Argyle Park, and Grandview

(Boulevard Place and Harkness Heights streets were not named until after the Denver City Ordinance of 1904 and have always borne present names.)

East-west:

Present name	Former name or names
West 38th Avenue	Prospect
West 39th Avenue	Cherry, Tweed, A
West 40th Avenue	not cut through
West 41st Avenue	Maple, Tay, B
West 42nd Avenue not cut through in Berkeley;	Forth in Argyle Park
West 43rd Avenue	Oak, Clyde, C
West 44th Avenue	Jefferson, Dee, Burtis, Curtis, Gaston, D
West 45th Avenue	North Denver, Barnes, E
West Scott Place	Scott
West 46th Avenue	Walker, Taylor, F
West 47th	not cut through
West 48th Avenue	Lake, H
West 49th Avenue	Berkeley, I
West 50th Avenue	College, North Blvd., J
West 51st Avenue	Locust, K

North-south:

When east-west streets in Berkeley were changed to letters, the north-south streets, which had been numbered, were given the titles formerly used on the east-west:

Present name	Former name or names
Federal	Boulevard, Boulevard F
Green Court	8th, Wellesley
Grove	9th, Bleecher, Flack in Grand View
Hooker	10th, Canby, Beacon in Grand View
Irving	11th, Edward, Bosler in Grand View
Julian	12th, Austin
Knox Court	Tyndall, McClain in Grand View
King	Loyola, Mackey in Grand View
Lowell	13th, Berkeley, Schiller, Homer Shaw in Grand View
Meade	14th, Ewing
Newton	15th, Anne
Osceola	16th, Cary
Perry	17th, Sterling
Quitman	18th, Inverness
Raleigh	19th, Lorne
Stuart	20th, Dumbarton
Tennyson	21st, Canby, Lake
Utica	22nd, Water
Vrain	23rd, North
Winona Court	24th, Oak
Wolff	25th, Park
Xavier	26th, Locust
Yates	27th, Maple
Zenobia	28th, Cherry

Bibliography

Books

Arps, Louisa Ward. *Denver in Slices.* Denver: Sage Books, 1959.

Bird, Isabella L. *A Lady's Life in the Rocky Mountains.* The Western Frontier Library. Norman: University of Oklahoma Press, 1966.

Bretell, Richard R. *Historic Denver: The Architects and the Architecture.* Denver: Historic Denver, Inc., 1973.

Burt, S. W. and Berthoud, E. L. *Rocky Mountain Gold Regions.* Denver City, J.T. (Jefferson Territory): Rocky Mountain News Printing Co., 1861.

Byers, William N. *History of Colorado, Vol. 1.* Chicago: Century Publishing and Engraving Co., 1901.

Denver City and Auraria, The Commercial Emporium of the Pikes Peak Gold Regions in 1859. St. Louis (?): 1860.

Denver City Directories, 1873-1950.

Dier, Caroline Lawrence. *The Lady of the Gardens.* Hollywood: Hollycrofters, Inc., Ltd., 1932.

Ferril, William C. *Sketches of Colorado.* Western Press Bureau Co., 1911.

Fowler, Gene. *Timberline: A Story of Bonfils and Tammen.* Garden City, New York: Blue Ribbon Books, 1940.

Francis, Harriet E. *Across the Meridians.* The DeVinne Press, 1887.

Griswold, Don and Jean. *Colorado's Century of "Cities".* Denver: Smith Brooks Printing Co., 1958.

Hall, Frank. *History of Colorado, Vols. 3, 4.* Chicago: Blakely Printing Co., 1895.

Jones, William C.; Wagner, F. Hol, Jr.; and McKeever, Gene C. *Mile-High Trolleys.* Denver: Bradford-Robinson Printing Co., 1965.

King, Clyde Lyndon. *The History of the Government of Denver with Special Reference to Its Relations with Public Service Corporations.* Denver: Fisher Book Co., 1911.

Kostka, William. *The Pre-Prohibition History of Adolph Coors Co., 1873-1933.* Denver: 1973.

Larimer, William H. H. *Reminiscences of General William Larimer.* Printed for private circulation under the auspices of William Larimer Mellon. Reprinted Lancaster, Pa.: New Era Printing Co., 1958.

Long, Margaret. *The Smoky Hill Trail.* Denver: W. H. Kistler Stationery Co., 1943.

Parsons, Eugene. *The Making of Colorado.* Chicago: A. Flanagan Company, 1908.

Perilli, Giovanni, M.D. *Colorado and the Italians in Colorado.* Denver: 1922.

Perkin, Robert. *First Hundred Years.* Garden City, New York: Doubleday, 1959.

Semple, James Alexander, ed. *Representative Women of Colorado.* Denver: Alexander Art Publishing Co., Press of the Williamson-Haffner Co., 1911.

Smiley, Jerome. *History of Denver*. Denver: Denver Times and Times Sun Publishing Co., 1901.

Sprague, Marshall. *Newport in the Rockies*. Centennial Edition. Chicago: Swallow Press, Inc., 1971.

Stone, Wilbur Fiske. *History of Colorado, Vol. 1*. Chicago: S. J. Clarke Publishing Co., 1918.

Uchill, Ida Libert. *Pioneers, Peddlers and Tsadikim*. Denver: Sage Books, 1957.

Van Cise, Philip S. *Fighting the Underworld*, Second Edition. Cambridge, Massachusetts: The Riverside Press, 1936.

Vickers, William B. *History of Denver, Vol. 4*. Chicago: O. L. Baskin and Company, 1880.

Weeks, Lyman Horace. *Prominent Families of New York*. New York: The Historical Company, 1897.

Wharton, J. E. *The City of Denver from Its Earliest Settlement to Present Time, to which is added a full and complete business directory of the city by D. O. Wilhelm, Denver, Colorado*. Denver: Byers and Dailey, 1866. Reproduced by D. O. Wilhelm, Eastwood-Kirchner, 1909.

Woman's Who's Who of America. New York: American Commonwealth Co., 1914-1915.

Articles, Reports, and Pamphlets

Arps, Louisa Ward. "Travels of 'The Boy and a Frog'." *The Green Thumb*, July-August, 1966.

"City Golf Links." *City of Denver*, December 7, 1912.

Committee of the Colorado Scientific Society. Report by the Commission on *Artesian Wells of Denver*. Denver: 1884.

DeBoer, S. R. "Plans, Parks and People." *The Green Thumb*, December, 1972.

DeConde, Alexander. "To the Land of Promise: The Italian Exodus to America." *American History Illustrated*, August, 1972.

Denver Public Schools, Division of School and Business Services. "The Next 6 Years: A School Building Program Designed to Improve Educational Facilities in the Denver Public Schools." Denver: January, 1976.

Eberhart, Perry. "Brick Pomeroy — Fabulous Failure." *Empire Magazine*, July 5, 1959.

"Fortunes in Colorado." *St. Louis Magazine*, October, 1881.

Highlands, City of. *Dedication Brochure of City Hall, 1890*.

History of Holy Family Church, Golden Jubilee, 1905-1955.

Kassler and Co. *All in the Company*. October, 1972.

Lupton, F. M. *Handy Cyclopaedia of Every-Day Wants*, The People's Hand Book Series, New York: 1893.

Peabody, Olive. *Birth of a Hospital*. Denver.

————. *The Oakes Home, A Haven of Peace*. 1931.

Robertson, Clyde. "Biography of Lillian White Spencer." *American Poetry Journal*, January, 1934.

Stanchfield, E. E. "Song of the San Juan: Memoirs of Early Colorado." 1949.

U. S. Department of State Register, January 1, 1932.

Woodward, Wes. "M. Walter Pesman: He Made the Native Plants Our Friends." *The Green Thumb*, Autumn, 1975.

Manuscripts and Unpublished Materials

Board of Aldermen, City of Highlands, Arapahoe County, Colorado. Minutes of Meetings, 1875-1876. Colorado State Archives.

Board of Directors, Rocky Mountain Ditch Company. Minutes of Meetings, Vol. 3 1880-1889, Vol. 4 1890-1919.

Board of Trustees, Town of Argo, Arapahoe County, Colorado. Minutes of Meetings, 1879-1903. Colorado State Archives.

Bromwell, Henrietta E., ed. "Colorado Portrait and Biography Index." Denver Public Library, 1931, 1932, 1933.

City Council, Town of North Denver [Berkeley], Arapahoe County, Colorado. Minutes of Meetings, 1892-1903. Colorado State Archives.

Clarke, Perry, L. "Noted and Historical Trees in and around Denver, Colorado." Colorado State Forestry Association, 1934.

Denver Department of Parks and Recreation. "History of Development, Denver City Parks."

Denver Planning Commission. "Community Renewal Program Analysis, 1950-60."

Documentary Resources. Research collection #305. Henry, Frederick William. State Historical Society of Colorado.

Draper, Ben, ed. "History of Denver's Parks." Document Division, Denver Museum Collection, 1934.

Feely, The Reverend Thomas. "The Catholic Church on the Early Colorado Frontier." Unpublished PhD dissertation, University of Denver, 1973.

Hansen, James E. II. "Prohibition in Denver." Unpublished M.A. thesis, University of Denver, 1965.

Letter from Office of the Postmaster General to Postmaster, Denver, Colorado, attention E. Sanelli. October 11, 1972.

Mosley, Earl L. *"History of the Denver Water System 1880-1919."* Denver Board of Water Commissioners.

"Sketch of Historic Landmark Church." Asbury United Methodist Church, 1975.

Spalding, Elizabeth. Scrapbook of the Artists Club of Denver and Denver Art Association, 1909-1919. Manuscript Collection, Western History Department, Denver Public Library.

Trimble, Anna G., ed. "Origin of Denver Streets." Denver Public Library, 1932.

Newspapers and Periodicals

Colorado Exchange Journal
Colorado Springs Gazette
Denver *Catholic Register*
Denver *Daily News*
Denver Daily Tribune
Denver Post
Denver Republican
Denver *Rocky Mountain News*
Denver Times
Denver Weekly Tribune
Grand Junction Sentinel
Jefferson County Republican
New York *Frank Leslie's Illustrated Newspaper*
Mountain and Plains Notes
Pueblo Star-Chieftain
Trinidad *Chronicle News*
Western Architect and Building News

Maps and Documents

Abstract of Title to 2438 Federal Boulevard, Denver, Colorado.

Abstract of Title to 2952-56 Wyandot Street, Denver, Colorado.

Baist, C. William and H. V. "Atlas of the City of Denver, Colorado." Philadelphia, 1905.

Denver Lithographic Co. "Map of Denver." Colorado Real Estate Exchange, Denver, 1890 (?).

Highland Park original plat as filed with Clerk and Recorder of Arapahoe County, Territory of Colorado, May 28, 1875.

Highland Park, vacation of portion of original plat, as filed with Clerk and Recorder, Arapahoe County, Colorado, September 1, 1887.

Ordinances of City of Highlands, Colorado, 1889.

Robinson, Elisha. "Atlas of the City of Denver, Colorado." New York: 1887.

Rollandet, Edward. "Map of the City of Denver, Arapahoe County, State of Colorado." Denver: 1885.

Sanborn Map Co., Ltd. "Real Estate Atlas, Vol. 3." New York: reprinted 1929.

Index

Italic indicates illustrations

Suggested Tours

Tour #1 is a short one, between three and four miles long, and takes you through one of the oldest parts of the city, where the residents are working diligently with city agencies and commissions to preserve what is good. It is an area where business, industry, and freeways are encroaching on residential sections, with resultant decay of some buildings. But it is also an area of small fascinating Victorian cottages, landmark churches, and many sizable and substantial historical residences, with well kept lawns, trees, flowers, and ornamental fences.

Tour #2 is a longer one of about fifteen miles, which winds through West Colfax, Highlands, Berkeley, and part of Argyle Park, and takes you to three of Denver's parks. You will find a little decay, but the residences range from cottages to near-mansions, including several landmark houses. There are small business and retail outlets along arterial streets.

As you look at the buildings, keep in mind that the architects and builders of the 80's and 90's seemed to want you to look up. They decorated tops — tops of windows, tops of porches, bargeboards of the houses. Notice the dormers and bay windows, the fanciful arrangements of shingles on the facades of the gables of cottages, elaborate brickwork along the cornice of flat roofed buildings, or the scrolled eaves brackets of villa-type homes.

On both tours, please look, but *don't* intrude on the privacy of homes or grounds.

Have a good time, and come back soon to see more on the side streets and byways.

Self-Conducted Tour #1: Original North Denver and Eastern Highlands

Come to Northwest Denver via 15th Street viaduct. Notice new Platte River Park where Denver, Auraria, and Highland started (p. 48). Alternate route: 16th Street viaduct, turning left at north end onto Central Street.

Drive or walk the one block of 15th Street from Central to Boulder (p. 24), earliest business section. Notice cast iron front pilasters. The section now is devoted to arts and crafts galleries and coffee houses. The old North Denver Bank, which was the King-McDowell Building (p. 25, 26) burned during September, 1976.

Drive north to the 5-way intersection of 15th, West 29th, Boulder, and Umatilla (traffic light.) Make a sharp left to Umatilla, go one block to West 28th Avenue, right on 28th to see unusual brownstone townhouses with unique stone carvings on left side of this block (p. 28).

Continue on West 28th to Wyandot, turn right. Wheeler house at southwest corner (p. 15). Tallmadge and Boyer terraces and grocery on west side (left) of Wyandot between 29th and 30th (p. 32).

Turn right on W. 30th to Asbury United Methodist Church at Vallejo Street (one block) (p. 37). Left on Vallejo, drive north one block, west one block to Wyandot, north on Wyandot to West 32nd Avenue to see Chapel of Our Merciful Savior (All Saints Episcopal Church) (p. 35).

Left on West 32nd Avenue, past old business section at 32nd and Zuni, including Weir Building (p. 76). Notice white brick house at 2533 West 32nd Avenue, oldest house shown on inventory of North Denver, built in 1872.

Turn right at Bryant. Directly behind you on West 32nd is the Thomas Ward home (p. 72). James A. Fisher house on left at 3227 Bryant, with large carriage house and brick wall (p. 73, 74). Frank Arbuckle frame residence at 3257 Bryant (p. 57).

Proceed north to 34th and Bryant. Notice gingerbread porches on house at southeast corner of intersection. Church of God, formerly Highland Christian Church, built in 1903, on northwest corner.

Turn right on 34th (interesting houses in this block). Pass Mackay (graystone landmark) at southwest corner of Alcott Street and 34th (p. 96). Continue east on 34th to Zuni (one block.)

Left on Zuni to 36th, right on 36th to Osage, passing North Side Community Center, southwest corner of 36th and Pecos. Left on Osage, to see the Damascio house at 3611-15 Osage (p. 43).

Continue to West 37th, turn right one block to Navajo. Right on Navajo to 36th. Mount Carmel Italian Catholic Church on southwest corner (p. 41).

Left on 36th to Kalamath, to Our Lady of Guadalupe Church (p. 47). Also notice the parish house across 36th, with lighted replica of Aztec calendar stone.

Right on Kalamath to 34th. Right on 34th. Notary House, where Mother Cabrini started convent, on southwest corner, 34th and Navajo (p. 40). One of North Denver's well known Italian restaurants, Little Pepina's, 34th and Osage.

Here you have a choice of how to return home. Turn right on Osage (one way street) to West 38th Avenue, turn right on 38th, which will lead you to Valley Highway or 23rd Street viaduct. Or continue on 34th one block to Pecos (one way) and turn left. This takes you past St. Patrick's Church at the corner of West 33rd. Turn left on 33rd, which brings you to 20th Street viaduct, (past original St. Patrick's church building, now occupied by Mexican Cafe). Or continue on 34th to Tejon, turn left, which will lead you to 16th Street viaduct. Or continue on 34th to Zuni, turn left, which will lead you to Speer viaduct or Valley Highway.

Self-Conducted Tour #2: West Colfax, Highlands, Berkeley, Argyle Park

Take West Colfax (Larimer) viaduct and Avenue to Stuart Street. Left on Stuart to 14th Street. There are five sizable houses here of the Voorhees addition (p. 157-161).

West on 14th Avenue to Tennyson (one block.) North (right) on Tennyson, crossing Colfax Avenue at traffic light. You are now in the former Highlands. You will pass Colfax Elementary School (p. 67) and the Hebrew Educational Alliance Synagogue. Left on 16th Avenue to Yates, to see Gustav Winter house at 1575 Yates (southwest corner), with its fanciful iron work (p. 122).

North (right) on Yates to Sloan's Park. A good spot for a picnic. Try to visualize Manhattan Beach across the lake at the northwest corner (p. 143).

If you wish, turn west to Sheridan, follow Sheridan to traffic light at West Byron Place (in Denver) or West 25th Avenue (in Edgewater on the left). Turn right and follow road around lake to 18th Avenue and turn north on Meade Street. Or you may leave the park and turn east directly onto 17th Avenue, passing back of St. Anthony's Hospital. Turn left (north) on Meade to 21st, east on 21st to Hooker, passing CARIH National Asthma Center. At northwest corner of 21st and Hooker Street is landmark house, beautifully restored by Congressman Tim Wirth (p. 152).

Right on Hooker one block to 20th, left on 20th one block to Grove. Walk or drive *slowly* north the two blocks between 20th and 22nd on Grove so that you may enjoy every house on each side of the street, and also those west of Grove on West 22nd Avenue. Landmark house at 2143 Grove (p. 99 and cover).

Drive north on Grove Street, passing 2401 Grove, another house being restored. It is built in angles, and few rooms in the house have four square corners. North to 26th, west (left) to Hazel Court, to 27th.

Turn right on 27th, to Grove Street. This is in the middle of the Kennedy farm, where the Sells-Floto winter quarters were (p. 151). Turn left (north) on Grove, to drive past the Kennedy farmhouse at 2727 Grove (p. 93).

Left at 28th to Irving, right at West 26th Avenue. Follow West 26th to Perry Street. North on Perry. At 2841 and 2851 Perry you will pass two identical (on the exterior) charming Victorian houses, both of which were owned by Frank Woodbury, General Roger W. Woodbury's son. The corner one is still in the hands of the family.

Continue north up the hill on Perry. Notice the red sandstone two story house at 2954 Perry. It is trimmed with white sandstone, a reversal of most structures. The half six-pointed star window lintels are very unusual (p. 196).

On your left is the large Carter house (p. 120).

At the northwest corner of West 30th and Perry is the Moses house, with its charming third floor balcony and tall oak tree (p. 108).

Turn right on 30th. At 30th and Osceola (one block) is the imposing Herman H. Heiser house, behind tall spruce trees on the northeast corner (p. 107). This is a landmark house.

One block farther east at Newton and 30th is the Wolff residence (p. 109). On your right is Little Sisters of the Poor Mullen Home for the Aged.

Continue two more blocks east to Lowell Boulevard. At the northwest corner of 30th and Lowell is the Ellis-Schenck residence (p. 116).

Turn left (north) on Lowell. This is the block of so many prominent people including Mayor Stapleton (p. 117). Continue north on Lowell. At 3417 and 3425 Lowell are the two Cox landmark houses (p. 110-112).

Turn left onto 35th, drive two blocks to Newton, right on Newton. At 3520 Newton is the Walker stone residence (p. 113). Continue to 38th, and turn left.

West on 38th, passing Ladies Relief Society (p. 185) on right side of 38th between Quitman and Raleigh, and the Mulvihill-Gurtler home at northwest corner of 38th and Raleigh (p. 186). Continue west on 38th, past Elitch Gardens on left (p. 131-139).

At Wolff Street (traffic light) turn right. You are now in Berkeley. Wander a bit if you want — wherever you spot tall trees or high roofs. Who knows, you might discover one of the thirty-five houses William Lang designed, or at least some copied after his style or that of other well-known Victorian architects (p. 166, 167).

Turn left on West 45th Avenue to Yates, to see the former Berkeley Post Office and City Hall at southeast corner of 45th and Yates (p. 170).

Continue in a northerly direction (right) until you come to West 46th Avenue. Here, if you have time, go left to Sheridan, right on Sheridan to Inspiration Point, and drive circle trip to top of point.

There are only a few entrances into Berkeley Park. We suggest the one off Tennyson (east side of park) at West 48th, just before you go under I-70. From here you can see the lake with the mountains, and Lakeside's tower, as backdrops.

Continue up the hill (north) on Tennyson, passing between Willis Case Golf Course on the left and some very attractive homes on the right. At West 50th Avenue, two blocks to your left (west) you will see the Masonic El Jebel Mosque.

Turn right on either West 50th Avenue or go over the hill to West 52nd, the city limits between Denver and Adams County. Drive east to Lowell Boulevard. (This is still part of the old town of Berkeley.) At Lowell turn right (south). On the northeast is Regis College. (p. 166).

At West 46th Avenue you may want to turn west to Perry (four blocks) to see the John McDonough Mediterranean style villa (p. 186-188). Then return to 46th Avenue, eastbound, driving between Rocky Mountain Lake (p. 9, 182), and some more attractive homes.

At Federal, either turn left to I-70 to return home; or preferably, turn right (south) on Federal, eighteen blocks to West 29th Avenue, passing many attractive homes, Masonic Temple, churches, Highland Park with Woodbury Library (p. 80), Knights of Pythias Hall. As you cross Speer Boulevard, you can see North High School half a block to your left (p. 66).

Turn east (left) on West 29th Avenue. In this first block, right hand side, at 2914 West 29th Avenue, is the Queree residence (p. 121).

At next corner, Eliot, turn right, past other interesting houses and the new Career Education Center of the Denver Public Schools.

Turn left at West 26th Avenue. On your left at 2637 West 26th is the former Dunwoody residence (p. 87, 88), now La Loma Restaurant.

Two blocks east is Diamond Hill (p. 78, 79), the former Roger W. Woodbury estate. One block to your left on Zuni Street you may take either Speer Viaduct or the Valley Highway to return home.